Sifted Like Wheat

WALKING WITH PETER
THROUGH THE GOSPELS

By Carla Holiday

Copyright © 2025 Carla Holiday

All rights reserved. No part of this book may be reproduced in any form without permission from the author or publisher, except as permitted by U. S. copyright law.

*To the ladies of my discipleship group
for their unending moral and spiritual support:
Ruth, Kristi and Helen*

*And to Rhonda,
Words cannot express my gratitude to you
for helping me fine-tune and finish this book.
Two are definitely better than one!*

Ecclesiastes 4:9-10

Table of Contents

Peter in the Gospels

Introduction 1

Chapter 1: The Call 7

Chapter 2: The Storm 21

Chapter 3: The Rock 35

Chapter 4: The Rebuke 49

Chapter 5: The Mountain 61

Chapter 6: The Cost 75

Chapter 7: The Refusal 89

Chapter 8: The Vow 103

Chapter 9: The Garden 117

Chapter 10: The Impulse 131

Chapter 11: The Denial 145

Chapter 12: The Renewal 161

Appendices 175

Introduction

Why Peter?

I'll be honest with you. Peter was never my favorite Bible personality. Not even close. He actually annoyed me quite frequently. I preferred someone more like Paul, an intellectual giant with an unwavering ambition to serve Christ, even if it killed him. And eventually it did.

To me, Peter always came off as more impulsive and unreliable, someone who might be fun to have a few laughs with, but I wouldn't trust him to keep his word or act responsibly. He would not be my "go-to" person.

Then something happened.

About 18 months ago, I was reading through the gospel of John a chapter a day, journaling my thoughts as I meditated on the passages. It wasn't until I reached the very last chapter of John that I noticed something about the relationship between Jesus and Peter that I had not seen before.

When I finished John, I continued through Acts. I found myself on several occasions stunned by the incredible transformation I saw in Peter. He was a changed man. The power with which he spoke to the crowds, the strength he exhibited in the face of opposition, the complete trust in God he demonstrated as he endured prison and persecution—this man Peter had experienced a radical transformation since he had traveled through Galilee learning from Jesus.

Even the high priest and his family, who had thought Peter uneducated and crude, were "astonished" when they heard him speak with confidence and courage (Acts 4:13, New International Version 1984).

What happened?

One obvious answer is that the Holy Spirit happened. From the time Jesus said, "Receive the Holy Spirit," to the fiery day of Pentecost, the presence of the Holy Spirit had a transformational impact on Peter and the other disciples.

Also, Peter had spent about 40 days learning from his now resurrected Lord, who I'm sure had a lot of teaching to pass on to his newly humbled yet overjoyed disciple. Hindsight is 20/20. Jesus had often said to his disciples when they were confused by his teaching, "You do not understand now, but you will later." I can almost hear Peter saying, "Oh, I get it now! That makes perfect sense!"

But what about the three years Peter spent traveling with Jesus, learning from him and witnessing miracles? What about all the moments he failed or spoke out of turn or contradicted his Lord? Did these moments play a part in growing Peter from a simple fisherman named Simon, to a spiritual giant who led thousands to the Lord?

I think so.

I think the words of Paul in his first letter to the Corinthians set a framework through which we can grasp a little more of what God was doing in Peter's life, way back when he was still known as Simon:

Brothers and sisters, think of what you were when you were called. Not many of you were wise by human standards; not many were influential; not many were of noble birth. But God chose the foolish things of the world to shame the wise; God chose the weak things of the world to shame the strong. God chose the lowly things of this world and the despised things—and the things that are not—to nullify the things that are, so that no one may boast before him (1 Cor. 1:26-29).

Through Jesus, God chose Peter. He was not wise, influential, or of noble birth. And I think, when we see God work through Peter, we also see what God *can do* and *is doing* through *us*.

And so my quest began to really study the man Peter from his calling through his last recorded conversation with Jesus in John 21. I focused on the significant events—the ones the gospel writers chose to provide extra details that they did not provide for other situations.

When studying anything in the gospels, it's important to look at all four to get the best idea of what actually occurred. Matthew, Mark, Luke and John don't always write the exact same details. They are four different men writing to four different audiences. Matthew and John were physically present for the events they wrote about. Mark wrote his gospel while attending Peter and wrote down Peter's recollection. Luke was more like an investigative reporter. He interviewed scores of eyewitnesses and spent considerable time verifying facts and establishing timelines (See Appendix A).

It is important to recognize the differing audiences and agendas each gospel writer has, because it helps explain why one writer will describe in-depth details on a certain event while another will not even mention it. For example, why do all four writers speak of Jesus walking on water during a storm, but only John relates *Peter's* attempt to walk on the water? Each gospel writer writes from his own perspective, with his own agenda, to his own unique audience.

For a more complete picture of what actually happened, I encourage you to read all the accounts which I have referenced at the beginning of each chapter.

I also encourage you not to be concerned by apparent inconsistencies or disagreements between accounts. God's Word is divinely inspired and is truthful. Shortly before his death, Peter himself wrote that Scripture, though written by men, had its origin in God: "Men spoke from God as they were carried along by the Holy Spirit" (2 Pet 1:20-21).

Where a problem appears to exist, the problem is not with the text but with us. Where there are apparent discrepancies, I have endeavored to reconcile or harmonize the accounts without sacrificing the intent of the text. And even if our attempts at harmonization are misguided, God's Word is still true. We are the ones who are missing pieces and must trust that the full picture is wholly intact and one day will be revealed. God does not give us every detail of what happened every minute of every day; but he has given us all we *need* to know.

I have tried to be very clear about when I am making inferences or speculating, and when the text is sufficient on its own to paint a complete picture of what happened. As I read the gospel accounts, I have tried to put myself in Peter's shoes (or sandals). I bring myself into the context, with all my own weaknesses, thought patterns, likes and dislikes. I ask myself, what would I think in this situation? How would I feel if this happened to me? Why might I respond like Peter did?

While I am not Peter, and may respond differently than Peter, it does help me see more clearly through his eyes and understand his heart a little better. Peter becomes more alive to me and not just printed words on paper. He was a real man, living in a real world, dealing with some very unusual situations. I think it's important when reading the Bible, for all of us to picture ourselves in the historical context and ask ourselves honestly, *what would I do?*

And this is what made my perception of Peter change so drastically. When I actually walked with Peter and tried to see things from his perspective, I found myself able to identify with him, to understand just a little better why he did or said what he did. I realized that despite all his mistakes, all his impulsive words and actions, all his "foot in mouth" blunders, he stayed the course. Every time he took a step backwards, or three or four steps, he tried again.

I saw that through Peter's weaknesses, through his stumbles and falls, through his arrogant outbursts and panicked denials, Jesus never turned away from him. Jesus continued to forgive him, teach him, correct him, even rebuke him, and always encourage him.

And Peter never gave up. Often humbled, ashamed, and confused, he still pressed on to follow Jesus. When Jesus asked his disciples if they wanted to leave him like so many others had, Peter said, "Lord, to whom shall we go? You have the words of eternal life. We have come to believe and to know that you are the Holy One of God" (John 6:68-69). Despite all his failures, Peter knew whom he believed in.

I titled this book, *Sifted Like Wheat*, because that's what Peter's time with Jesus was like. In Luke 22:31, Jesus told Peter and the other disciples that Satan desired to sift them like wheat. During biblical times, sifting wheat was a process designed to remove chaff, dirt and other impurities from the edible grain. The wheat was placed in a sieve and then violently shaken. The agitation separated the good parts from the bad parts. Satan's desire was to violently shake up Peter and the other disciples in order to destroy their faith.

Sometimes being violently shaken is not a bad thing; it removes the impurities and leaves what is good. But it's also not a pleasant experience if *you are the wheat*. In looking at Peter's time with Jesus, we can see the difficulties he endured, we can cringe at the mistakes he made, we can rejoice at the times he spoke truth, but mostly we can be encouraged that he *kept coming back.*

Why Peter?

Of all the people he could have chosen, why did Jesus call this particular fisherman to be numbered among his closest disciples?

Because, in the end, we all have a little bit of Peter in us. We all face situations in which we say something stupid. We all stick our foot in our mouth. We all think we know better than others. We all deny Christ when we are embarrassed to acknowledge we know him. We all run away when we are scared.

But Jesus is here, as he was with Peter, to forgive us, correct us, rebuke us, and encourage us. Peter is our example. He is our picture of how one person can fail over and over again yet continue to receive the forgiveness and love of the Lord.

May we, like Peter, keep coming back.

Chapter 1

The Call

"Come, follow me," Jesus said,

"and I will make you fishers of men."

At once they left their nets and followed him.

Matthew 4:19-20

Read First:
Matthew 4:18-20; Mark 1:16-18; Luke 5:1-11; John 1:40-42

When we read the gospels, we are struck by two often extreme sides of Peter.

Peter. Leader. Charismatic. Top three disciple. Renamed "the Rock." Called "blessed" by Jesus. Given the "keys of God's kingdom." First disciple to confess Jesus as Lord. The one who proclaimed, "Even if I have to die with you, I will never deny you."

Peter. Headstrong. Prideful. Impulsive. Called "Satan" by Jesus. Controlling to a fault. First disciple to rebuke Jesus. The one who emphatically denied he even knew Jesus, let alone followed him.

Who was this man? How can both descriptions of Peter be right? How can one man be such a mix of opposite traits? Who was the real Peter?

We must start at the beginning, when he was still called Simon.

A Man Called Simon

As a young man in his early 20s, Simon was not much different than other men his age. In fact, he seemed fairly ordinary. Most men at that time married sometime in their late teens to early 20s. Simon lived with his wife, his brother Andrew, and his mother-in-law in the fishing village of Capernaum, about half mile from Lake Gennesaret, a freshwater lake also known as the Sea of Galilee.

He worked hard as a fisherman to support his family. He rose well before dawn. He fished all night. At the end of work, he looked forward to that moment when he could stretch out on his bed and exhale all the stress he accumulated during his waking hours. He slept. He ate. He took care of business at home. And then his day started over again. Every day just like the one before. Much like we experience.

Simon. An ordinary person. Yet this ordinary person collided with the extraordinary. He didn't expect it. He wasn't looking for it. But it still came. The moment of opportunity, the fork in the road, the call of God.

The First Call

The people of Israel were in "waiting mode." For hundreds of years they had been waiting for the promised Messiah, the savior from God who would free them from their political oppressors. On this man they pinned all their hopes for the future.

Simon's brother Andrew and their friend John were both students of John the Baptizer, a prophet who called for everyone to turn away from sin and be baptized.[1] He preached that the Messiah was coming very soon. He had been very clear that he himself was not the Messiah, but that the Messiah was near, even among them now. He described himself as simply someone who came before, to prepare the people for the true Messiah.

So, every day, as they learned from the Baptizer, Andrew and John eagerly listened for any clues about the identity of the Messiah.

Then one day, John the Baptist pointed Jesus out to his disciples. "Look, the Lamb of God, who takes away the sin of the world!" The following day, when he saw Jesus passing by, John the Baptist again said, "Look, the Lamb of God!" Here was the long-awaited Messiah.

Andrew and John went to Jesus immediately. They spent the day with him, listening to his teaching. How that teaching must have shaken them to the core, because by late afternoon, Andrew was convinced.

He ran to find his brother Simon. Breathless with excitement, he told him, "We have found the Messiah!"

It wasn't like Andrew to make dramatic claims without good reason. So Simon followed his brother straightaway, no hesitation. Perhaps he had already heard about this Jesus who was causing such a stir in the area. Maybe he had seen the crowds that Jesus attracted or had even heard him teach. Maybe he was just curious.

When Simon approached him, Jesus looked into his eyes and said, "You are Simon, son of John. You will be called Peter."

What?? Not the greeting Simon probably expected. What went through his head? Did Jesus' words catch Simon off-guard? Was he intrigued? Was he confused? What did he think when Jesus gave him a new name?

In the Scriptures, when God changed a person's name, it came with a new identity or mission. Simon would know that the name "Peter" meant "rock." Was he flattered? Was being called "rock" even a compliment? If so, was it a source of pride that this popular teacher singled him out in front of others? Whatever his thinking, his curiosity was aroused.

Could this man really be the Messiah?

A Night of Fishing

Simon (Peter) began following and learning from Jesus, along with his brother Andrew, and their fishing partners James and John. They were not alone. Jesus had a lot of followers. At this point, Jesus had not yet selected "Twelve" to be his closest disciples. Peter was simply one of many.

In the ensuing days, Jesus traveled north to Galilee with his followers. He visited his hometown of Nazareth and then attended a wedding in Cana where he performed his first miracle by turning water into wine.

Afterwards, Jesus walked to Capernaum, the home of Peter and Andrew, where he cast out a demon from a tormented man.[2] When Jesus learned that Peter's mother-in-law was suffering from a high fever, he went to her and healed her. Peter was present for both these miracles.

While in his hometown, Peter prepared for a night of fishing with Andrew. The small fishing town of Capernaum stirred to life at night; the best hauls came in still dark waters. In groups of twos and threes, the men of Capernaum made their way toward their boats and prepared to launch.

Peter likely gathered his gear, kissed his sleeping wife goodbye, and walked with Andrew to his fishing boat and loaded their equipment. Around them, other fishermen began casting off to make a living as well, including his fishing partners, James and John, the sons of Zebedee. The night air was crisp and the stars studded the sky with brilliant pinpoints of light.

Peter guided the boat into the deeper waters of the lake. He and Andrew hoisted the net over the side, hopeful for a good haul. Nearby, James and John did the same. Their families depended on a good catch to feed themselves, and to sell the rest to pay other expenses or buy necessary goods. But this night the fish were not cooperating. Over and over, they threw the net out and hauled it back into the boat.

No fish. Not even one.

As dawn approached, the brothers reluctantly made their way back to the shore. Tired and discouraged, they barely noticed the first rays of the rising sun streak the still dark sky.

They pulled their nets into the water just offshore to begin the difficult task of cleaning them of the endless plant life and other debris the nets always picked up. Cleaning the nets was particularly arduous when there was no catch to make it worth their while. What a wasted night.

No Ordinary Man

While washing their nets, Peter noticed a large crowd of people along the shore listening to a teacher. It was Jesus. The crowds were pressing in to hear him better. But the closer they pushed in, the less those in the back could see or hear. Peter kept watching as he cleaned, wishing he could hear what the teacher was saying.

Then Jesus saw Peter and began walking in his direction. Perhaps Peter nodded a greeting to Jesus only to be surprised when Jesus stepped onto his boat. His words caught Peter off-guard.

"Would you take me out on your boat a little way from the shoreline so I can better teach the people?" Jesus waited for Peter's answer.

Peter was tired. It had been a long failure of a night. He just wanted to go home and stretch out on his bed. But he knew Jesus was an influential man. He felt there was something different about him, something special. He didn't want to offend him. He could have made an excuse, tried to get out of helping Jesus, but he chose to do as Jesus requested.

So, Peter and Andrew cast off once again, positioning their boat where the people could better see and hear Jesus.

As Jesus continued teaching from the boat, Peter felt the weariness wash over him. He desperately needed sleep, but the teacher kept on speaking. When Jesus finally finished, Peter breathed a sigh of relief. But then Jesus turned to him once again and said,

"Now, let's go out into deeper water. And then let down your nets for a catch."

I imagine Peter hesitating, thinking, "Are you kidding me?" He was clearly irritated.

He had been up all night without catching any fish, and then he had spent most of the morning letting Jesus use his boat for a teaching session, and now he was being told to go out again, in the daylight, and fish? Who does that? Not anyone who knows how to fish!

Until this moment, Jesus had stayed in his lane, teaching the people about God and about the Scriptures. But now Jesus was straying into Peter's lane, fishing. This probably didn't sit well with him. He was the fisherman—not Jesus. He knew how to catch fish. His family had been fishing on this lake for generations. And he knew the fish were not biting. He knew sometimes you just have to call it a day. To go out again was a colossal waste of time. That this teacher had the nerve to tell him how to fish—

Peter's lips pressed together tightly as he restrained himself from saying what he really wanted to say. But it was hard to completely contain the testiness from his voice when he replied,

"Master, we've worked hard all night and haven't caught anything. But because you say so, I will let down the nets."

I've done that before—made sure everyone knows how much I have already done, how hard I've worked, and how unappreciated I am feeling, to cover up my own bad attitude toward someone else. It's hard to resist adding just a word or two to make certain the person knows that it's only out of the kindness of my heart that I'm doing this very nice thing for them, even though I think it's stupid or a waste of my time.

So, Peter and his brother begrudgingly set out from the shore into deeper waters. They tossed their nets over the leeward side of the boat, certain this was going to be a huge waste of time. Or so they thought...

No sooner had the nets broken the water's surface when the brothers felt the boat lurch sideways. Their eyes widened in astonishment. It couldn't be! Peter began pulling on the net. He struggled to raise it even a little—was it stuck on something? But the frantic splashing told a different story. Scores of wriggling silvery fish filled the nets to overflowing.

Peter had never seen so many fish in one haul. He and Andrew tried to pull the nets into the boat, but the massive number of fish was so heavy, they feared the nets would tear. The boat began to list sideways under the enormous weight. "We need help!" Peter shouted.

Andrew frantically waved down the Zebedee boys on shore to come to their aid. When their boat drew near, James and John quickly boarded the distressed boat and helped haul up the nets of fish.

When Peter's boat was filled to capacity, they began loading fish on the second boat, till it too was overflowing. All four were astonished at the huge catch. Enough fish to take care of their families for a long time. If even one more fish came aboard, they feared their boats would be in danger of sinking!

Throughout those few chaotic moments, Peter caught glimpses of Jesus sitting calmly, watching the men work. Peter's breathing became more rapid, and a sick feeling began to grow in his stomach. He knew, beyond a doubt, that this teacher was responsible for this incredible haul of fish. But that realization weighed him down rather than lifted him up.

At that moment, Peter remembered his words to Jesus, and the thoughts he had whispered in his heart. "Master, we've worked hard all night and haven't caught anything. But because *you* say so, I will let down the nets."

Oh, how he wished he could take back those words. He remembered the anger he had felt when Jesus asked him to fish again after a night of failure. He felt shame at his arrogant attitude, but he also felt heart-pounding fear like he had never felt before.

This man was no ordinary man, or even just a good teacher. This man was something far more. He not only had a grasp of the Scriptures, and taught in a way that stirred the heart, he had power to do what ordinary people could not. He had power even over the fish in the sea.

The Second Call

Who was this man? Was it possible that this was the Messiah?

Whoever he was, Peter knew he was in the presence of incredible wisdom, kindness and power. But Peter could not rejoice at that moment. Rather, remorse and shame pushed him down to his knees at the feet of Jesus. Recognizing the depravity of his own heart, he cried out in desperation, revealing the true nature of his earlier response to Jesus.

"Go away from me, Lord; I am a sinful man!"

Jesus looked with compassion on Peter. The one who could see all that was in the heart of a man touched Peter's shoulder and spoke with both authority and gentleness. He said,

"Don't be afraid; come, follow me." His eyes moved from Peter to include the other three men. "From now on you will be fishers of men."

And here, then, was the second call. The call to not merely follow him and learn from him, but to also work alongside him to reach people with the truth of who God is and how to have a right relationship with him.

Jesus not only called Peter and the others to a deeper commitment, he provided for their future needs with the huge haul of fish. When he calls, he does not leave us without provision—Jesus takes care of our needs as we move forward with him and trust him with our lives.

Trust sometimes means you may not know the details, but you step forward because you know the man.

I'm reminded of Jesus' words spoken later in his ministry, "Consider the birds of the air. They do not sow or reap or store away in barns, and yet your heavenly Father feeds them. Are you not much more valuable than they?"[3] Jesus called Peter and provided for his family and their future needs.

Peter now stood at the crossroads of his life. Would he choose the familiarity of the life he had always known, the life that was predictable and expected? Or would he take a risk, step into the unknown, the uncontrollable, and give the reins of his life to this man, this extraordinary man, who told him to set aside his fears and follow him?

Jesus saw the fear in Peter, the fear that would be an obstacle to his spiritual growth on more than one occasion in the future. Jesus said, put aside your fear. Trust me. Follow me. Look to me and I will lead you, teach you, take care of you and protect you. But you have to trust me. So, don't be afraid. Come. Follow me.

Surely questions formed in the mind of Peter. Follow him where? Follow him how long? These details were not addressed. But trust sometimes means you may not know the details, but you step forward because you know the man.

After the four men pulled their boats up on shore, they immediately left everything and followed him. And from that day forward, Peter's life changed dramatically.

Jesus had given Peter more than he imagined possible. More than he deserved. And times would come when Peter would not live up to the task. So many mistakes, so many failures. But that's what makes him so relatable.

If Jesus can call Peter, and then stand by him and teach him and encourage him and rebuke him and forgive him over and over again, does that not give us hope for ourselves?

Personal Reflection

Can you see yourself in Peter? I can. I see myself in every failure, in every misspoken word, in every missed opportunity, in every weakness and sin.

Jesus sees inside our hearts. He sees the doubt, the fear, the weakness, the shame, the sin, yet he says, "Come, follow me. I will take care of you. I will take care of your family. Don't be afraid. Come, follow me."

How are you like Peter? What is keeping you from following Christ wholeheartedly and without reservation?

Are you afraid of what the call really means? Are you anxious that Jesus will not be there for you when it counts the most? Is there something in your life that you are putting before Jesus--possessions, comfort, security, control of your own life?

Many are called, but few follow.

Jesus already knows what it is—you're not hiding anything from him. He knows you inside and out. He knows what motivates you and what scares you. He knows your deepest darkest secrets. Yet he still calls each of us to follow him.

Why? Because he loves us. He wants us to experience the joy that comes from following God. He wants us to be free from the burden of sin. And he wants us to join him in calling others.

What do you need to do to answer Christ's call to follow him?

What stands in your way? What fear holds you back? What questions do you need answered? Examine your heart and pour out your cares and concerns to God.

---

[1] It was common at that time for young men to spend a few years learning under a qualified teacher, in an apprentice-type relationship. The teacher's students were called "disciples." Though students, these men also worked to help support their families, while spending as much time as possible with their teacher.

[2] This is the first time the Bible records the casting out of a demon from a person.

[3] Matt. 6:26.

My Journal

Chapter 2

The Storm

But when he saw the wind, he was afraid and, beginning to sink, cried out,

"Lord, save me!"

Immediately Jesus reached out his hand and caught him.

"You of little faith," he said, "why did you doubt?"

Matthew 14:30-31

Read First:
Matthew 14:22-33; Mark 6:45-52; John 6:16-21

Have you ever been caught outside by a sudden storm?

I was driving home one evening from a friend's house. While there, I learned that a storm was heading towards us. I looked at the radar on my phone and figured I had just enough time to make it home before the storm hit. I jumped in my car and headed out.

I remember getting about halfway home when I was stopped by a red light at an overpass. While waiting for the light to change, I could hear the wind picking up. My car shook. Drops began to hit the windshield. Hurry up, light, I whispered anxiously. Was it always this long??

Then the deluge hit. The light changed just as sheets of water poured from the heavens and the wind threatened to push my car off the overpass. Visibility vanished. I slowed to a crawl, wipers on full blast, but couldn't see five feet in front of me. I began to pray for God's protection.

I inched my way forward for about two blocks and then made the decision to pull over and wait it out. I could hear the tornado sirens going off in the distance. It began to hail, bullets of ice smashing into my car as rivers of water rushed through the streets. The wind wreaked havoc, bending trees in half, stripping off their leaves.

I parked under a tree for a little protection from the rain but then wondered if that wasn't a terrible idea. I imagined the tree ripped from the ground and falling on my car. I prayed harder. The more the storm raged, the more I saw the damage around me, the easier it was to panic.

Finally, after about fifteen minutes, the storm began to abate. I slowly and carefully maneuvered my car around broken, mangled branches in the middle of the streets and standing water of unknown depths. I made it home. God had protected me.

Jesus' Early Ministry

The gospels tell of a time when Peter and the disciples also faced a terrible storm while sailing in the middle of Lake Galilee. Peter was still learning the ropes of what it meant to follow Jesus. In fact, Jesus had started his ministry only months earlier, when he was about thirty years old. That was the age that one could become a rabbi and begin teaching students. His ministry was initiated by his baptism in the Jordan River by his cousin John the Baptist.

Jesus had quite a few disciples following him early on. Young men were encouraged to learn from a qualified teacher in addition to making a living to support their family. This is likely what Peter and the other disciples did.

Peter and Andrew were originally from Bethsaida but were living about six miles away in a house in Capernaum with Peter's wife and his wife's mother when they began following Jesus. Capernaum was a fishing village, about a half mile from the lake. Several times in the gospels we read accounts of Jesus crossing over the Sea of Galilee to the other side and back. It may be that Peter's boat, or one belonging to James and John, was utilized during these trips.

Much of Jesus' ministry was in and around Capernaum. In fact, Jesus relocated from Nazareth to Capernaum shortly after preaching in the synagogue at Nazareth. Jesus' move to Capernaum occurred directly before the miraculous catch of fish described in the previous chapter, when Jesus said to Peter, "Come, follow me, and I will make you fishers of men."

The move brought about the fulfillment of a prophecy made by Isaiah, hundreds of years earlier, that the Messiah would arise by the Sea of Galilee, and that people living in darkness would be given a great light.[4]

Capernaum was strategically situated on a very popular trade route, making the fishing village a busy hub for commerce and travel. The people of the towns near Capernaum gathered with those passing through to listen to this teacher whose words rang with the authority of truth.

Mountains to the west and north, and the lake to the east, created a kind of amphitheater for teaching. Jesus often taught on the side of a mountain, or he set out in a boat a little offshore so that the crowds were between him and the mountains.

The open air between the crowds and him carried sound better than if both parties were on a flat surface. Also, the hard surfaces of the rock helped reflect the sound, amplifying it. Finally, the cooler breezes coming down the side of the mountains toward the lake helped carry sound. It was an ideal set-up for teaching large crowds of people.

The terrain also was ideal for sudden storms. The cooler air from higher in the mountains would rush downward to the lake. When it met the warmer air below, violent storms would often arise.

Fishermen knew it was dangerous to be caught by a storm while in the middle of the lake, so they tended to stay closer to shore to fish unless they were certain the weather would remain calm. When a storm did arise, a deep mist would settle over the raging waters, making visibility very dim.

Matthew, Mark and John's gospels all record a particularly violent storm that raged while the disciples were in a boat in the middle of the lake.

Prior to this storm, Peter and the others had been a part of Jesus' local and longer distance trips. They had witnessed the miracle of the water turning to wine in Cana. They had watched him overturn the tables of the moneychangers in Jerusalem the first time it happened. They were witnesses to the repentance of an entire town in Samaria.

They had seen the healing of the centurion's servant, Peter's mother-in-law, and a paralytic man. They had witnessed the raising of Jairus' daughter from the dead. They had watched him cast out demons and heal leprosy. They were no strangers to the miracles he performed and the lives he changed.

So sometimes it's hard to understand how they so easily gave in to fear when their circumstances became difficult. Particularly after this significant day...

The Storm

It had been a long day of teaching. The huge crowd of 5000 men, some with families, were hungry, yet the disciples only had a couple of fish and a few loaves of bread. They were astounded when Jesus multiplied their meager rations and fed the 5000.

As the crowd dispersed, Jesus told the disciples to get into the boat and sail to the other side of the lake. He wanted some time alone to pray. He walked up the side of a mountain and spent time speaking with his Father.

When the sun was dipping low in the sky, Jesus could see the boat in the middle of the lake. A sudden storm had sprung up over the water. The waves of the lake grew strong and wild. The wind pushed the boat farther into deeper waters, about four miles from the shore. The disciples were straining to row and gain control of the boat, but the waves continued to rise and crash all around them.

I can imagine Peter, soaked through, barking out orders in the chaos of that voyage, trying to regain control of the boat. They continued to fight the storm until sometime between three and six in the morning. They must have been exhausted, bailing water, trying to stay afloat.

And that's when they saw him. Walking on the water. Towards them.

Peter and the others were utterly terrified. Even after all the miracles, all the time they had spent with their Teacher, all their talk of him being the Messiah, this demonstration of power left them shaking with fear and doubt. "It's a ghost!" They cried out, panic in their voices. Perhaps the mist off the water obscured their vision. Immediately, when Jesus saw their fear, he called out to them,

"Take courage! It is I. Do not be afraid."

What did Peter feel when he realized that the figure was not a ghost, but actually Jesus? What thoughts ran through his head? Did he react out of pure emotion, without thought? He may have experienced a surge of elation, realizing that this truly is the Son of God. Who else could do such miraculous things?

He leaned over the still heaving side of the boat and shouted out to Jesus, "Lord, if it is You, command me to come to You on the water."

Peter's response is telling. Jesus had just told them all, "It is I." Yet Peter's words indicate he still had a measure of doubt. Is it you? Really? Then give me a sign. Give me the same power that you are manifesting right now.

Now, remember, *just one day earlier* Peter had witnessed the miraculous feeding of the 5000. Over the previous months, he had watched Jesus heal numerous people, including his own mother-in-law from a dangerously high fever. He had seen demons cast out, and water turned into wine. What could have prompted this request to his Lord?

Now, I don't know what Peter was thinking at that moment, or if he was even thinking. I try to picture myself in that situation. I don't think I would have asked to walk on water, nor would I have even wanted to walk on water. But perhaps that points to my own lack of faith.

I can imagine some possible reasons Peter would tell Jesus to command him to come to him on the water. Maybe he was compelled by a surge of euphoria (or adrenaline). Maybe walking on water just looked really cool. Maybe he wanted to impress the other disciples with his bravery. Maybe he really just wanted to be with Jesus.

Peter said, "If it is you...!"

I have trouble with those words.

When God tells us something quite plainly, and then we question it, we reveal a weakness in our own faith, in our ability to fully trust God.

For example, when God plainly told Adam, "You are free to eat from any tree in the garden; but you must not eat from the tree of the knowledge of good and evil, for when you eat of it you will certainly die," Satan questioned God's declaration.

"Did God really say, 'You must not eat from any tree in the garden'?"

Eve replied, "We may eat fruit from the trees in the garden, but God did say, "You must not eat fruit from the tree that is in the middle of the garden, and you must not touch it, or you will die."

Satan replied, "You will certainly not die..."

Adam and Eve doubted God's word and acted against the one very simple command God had given them, and all humanity suffered for it.[5]

Jesus told Peter, "It is I."

Peter replied, "If it is you..." and then asked for a sign, proof that Jesus was who he said he was.

How much more proof did Peter need than what he had already witnessed these past months?

I imagine the other disciples watching intently, holding their breath, not knowing what might happen next. Over the roar of the waves and the howling wind, they hear Jesus' response to Peter.

"Come."

The Moment of Testing

Did Peter's heart stop for just a second? Did the full impact of his request and Jesus' answer finally hit him? Now is the moment of testing. Now is the time when what Peter *said* he believed and what he *really* believes will be revealed to all. It's all on the line. What was really inside Peter's heart?

If you're going to commit to a course of action, it's important to be one hundred percent committed. That commitment is rooted in a choice, rather than on feelings or adrenaline. Adrenaline will only carry you so far before it will dissipate and abandon you. That's when the faith that you say you have will either manifest itself, or you will show the world that your claim to faith is not as strong as you thought.

Likely, Peter's adrenaline took him over the side of the boat. As he kept his eyes on Jesus, his feet made contact with the crashing waves, and he actually took a few steps toward Jesus.

But Matthew's gospel tells us that when he saw the power of the wind, when he heard the roar of the waves, when he felt the black pit of fear in his gut, when the dark clouds of doubt blocked Jesus from his sight, he began to sink.

Now, here's what I think happened. I think Peter acted purely on emotion. I think Jesus *allowed* him to exit the boat as an opportunity to show Peter the *real* state of his heart. I don't think Peter's faith sustained him through even those first couple of steps. Jesus held him afloat the second his feet hit the water.

Jesus is saying, "You can do nothing without me. I am your source of strength. I am your only hope. Your enthusiasm, your intelligence, your physical aptitude, your talent, your ambition, your resources, your will—nothing you have in yourself is able to sustain you in the storm. I alone am your Savior. Salvation is found only in me."

"Lord, save me!" Peter cried out.

Yes, these are the words our hearts must repeatedly cry whether we are in the middle of the storm or dealing with the challenges of an ordinary day.

Immediately Jesus reached out His hand and took hold of Peter.

Immediately.

The help came first; then the lesson.

Jesus didn't let Peter drown. He didn't even let him cough up a little water. Immediately, Jesus took hold of Peter.

Why? Jesus knows what we are like. He knows that we are weak. He knows that we will fail. He knows that we think more highly of ourselves than we ought. He sees our need to be in control. He sees the deceitfulness of our own hearts. He knows that we are both the *helpless sheep* in need of guidance and discipline, and we are the *prodigal son*, stubbornly insisting that we are the boss of our own lives, and can manage alone, thank you very much.

Yet he is always ready with an open hand when we call out to him. "As a father has compassion on his children, so the Lord has compassion on those who fear him; for he knows how we are formed, he remembers that we are dust."[6]

Likewise, when praying in the Garden of Gethsemane shortly before his arrest, Jesus warned Peter, James and John, "Watch and pray so that you will not enter into temptation. For the spirit is willing, but the body is weak."[7]

He knows us. Through and through. He knows our hearts. He knows our thoughts. He knows our temptations and our failures. He empathizes with our weaknesses, because he himself was tempted in every way, just like us, but did not sin.[8] Yet he holds out his hand, ready to help immediately when we call on him. And we can be confident that his help is filled with mercy and grace.

Peter's journey is our journey. If Jesus can choose him and change him into a totally different man, what can he do with us?

How relieved Peter must have felt when Jesus' hand took hold of his, lifting him out of the choppy waters and to the safety of the boat.

The help came first; then the lesson.

Jesus does not let us off with a "Children will be children." No, though he recognizes our weakness, he also knows that if we keep our eyes on him, if we rely on his strength and don't allow ourselves to be distracted by the problems that confront us, if we follow where he leads, if we remember who he is, we will experience the fullness of life without fear and without doubt.

Just as he said to Peter, he also says to us:

"You of little faith," He said, "why did you doubt?"

Jesus identified Peter's problem. His faith was small. In that moment, Peter doubted that Jesus was truly God.

You of Little Faith

I cannot talk about Peter without acknowledging that his problem is also my problem. Any time I don't take God at his word, any time I give in to fear, any time I think I can live as a Christian in my own strength, and don't give him credit for every breath that I take each day, I am revealing the smallness of my faith.

Not long before Peter's rescue, he and the disciples had been in a boat together with Jesus when another terrible storm had threatened to sink the boat. The waves swept over the side, and the disciples feared for their lives. All the while, Jesus slept through the storm.

That time, the disciples cried out, "Lord, save us! We're going to drown!"

Jesus woke up and rebuked the winds and waves, and the lake became calm. Turning to the disciples, he said, "You of little faith, why are you so afraid?" The men, amazed at what Jesus had done, exclaimed, "What kind of man is this? Even the winds and the waves obey him!"[9]

If we truly believe Jesus is the Son of God, why do we then doubt? Why do we fear? Why do we hesitate to do what he asks?

When Jesus climbed into the boat with Peter, the wind died down. No one should have been surprised. However, Mark's account of the story says that "the disciples were utterly astounded, for they had not understood about the loaves, but their hearts had been hardened."

They had not understood about the loaves.

Wait. What?

What had they not understood about the loaves? Why were their hearts hardened?

Keep reading! We will talk about that in Chapter Three. For now, it's safe to say that according to John's account, once the wind died down and the storm was calmed, those in the boat worshiped Jesus and proclaimed him to be the Son of God.

Personal Reflection

Peter is sometimes referred to as the "everyman" because in him we easily see ourselves.

He's impulsive and headstrong, easily moved to action, a natural leader who struggles with following, a man given to joyous highs who can also plummet to guilt-ridden lows. But through it all, he keeps moving forward, step by step, mistake after terrible mistake.

His journey is our journey. If Jesus can choose him and change him into a totally different man, what can he do with us?

How are you like Peter?

Are there things God wants you to do, that you have put on hold? Why?

How often do you ask Jesus for help? How often to you thank him for providing your every breath? In what area do you need to step out in faith and trust God to help you?

Like Peter, we cannot do anything without Jesus. He is our strength, he is our courage. But it's easy to say with all sincerity, "Truly, you are the son of God," and then still fear.

Head knowledge alone does not translate into faith.

James, Jesus' brother and later leader of the early church, wrote, "faith by itself, if it is not accompanied by action, is dead...Show me your faith without deeds, and I will show you my faith by my deeds. You believe that there is one God. Good! Even the demons believe that—and shudder."[10]

The demons have knowledge. They believe that Jesus is real. Yet they shudder in fear—their knowledge is not enough.

Faith is acting on the truth, and trusting the one who said, "I am the way, the truth, and the life. No one comes to the Father except through me."[11] How can you step out in faith in your own life?

---

[4] Matt. 4:12-16; Isa 9:1-2.

[5] Gen. 2:16-17; 3:1-4.

[6] Ps. 103:13-14.

[7] Matt. 26:41.

[8] Heb. 4:15.
[9] Matt. 8:25-27.
[10] James 2:17-19.
[11] John 14:6.

My Journal

Chapter 3

The Rock

"But what about you?" Jesus asked. "Who do you say I am?"

Simon Peter answered, "You are the Christ, the Son of the living God."

Matthew 16:15-16

Read First:
Matthew 16:13-20; Mark 8:27-30; Luke 9:18-20; John 6:22-69

We all have good days and bad days. Peter did as well. Perhaps his enthusiasm outweighed his faith when he tried to walk on the water. Only Matthew's gospel gave us the whole scoop on Peter's adventure. The other three focused solely on Jesus. Probably not Peter's best day...

But let's back up to the day before the huge storm. The loaves.

That morning, Jesus received word that his cousin John the Baptist had been killed by King Herod. Grieving, Jesus went out in a boat to spend time alone with his Father.

Though he had known this day would come, his heart ached for John. He turned to his Father for comfort, wisdom and guidance. With John gone, he knew all attention would now be directed solely at him.

As the people discovered that Jesus was alone in the boat, they gathered on the shore and waited for him, bringing their own personal needs and carrying their sick for him to heal.

When Jesus arrived and saw all the people, he was filled with compassion. He moved among them, healing their sick, and encouraging and comforting the hurting. It appears that he ministered to the crowds for the entire day.

By evening, the disciples suggested that Jesus tell the crowds to leave. It was growing dark, and they were a good walking distance from any town or village. If the people were going to buy food for themselves, they needed to get started. But Jesus had other plans.

"You give them something to eat," Jesus told them.

What was he thinking?

Some of the disciples had been grieving John's death as well. Some had been close followers and friends of John's. They also must have realized that with John gone, Jesus would now become the main target of interest among those who were envious of his popularity or opposed to his message. And if Jesus were a target, by extension, they also would be under suspicion.

On top of all these thoughts and emotions, they had just spent the entire day caring for a huge crowd of people—about 5000 men plus their families. The disciples were likely discouraged, tired, and hungry, and just wanted everyone to go away so that they could commiserate with one another. Alone. That's what I would want. Just a moment of peace.

"You give them something to eat."

When those words hit home, they were met with a rush of excuses.

"Should we go out and spend two hundred times a day's wage to give all of them bread to eat?"

I can imagine this probably came from Judas, since we know he handled the money for the group, and he was overly concerned with how the money was used.

"That would not buy enough bread for each of them to even have a small piece," Phillip declared.

"We have here only five loaves of bread and two fish," another pointed out.

"What *difference* will that make among so many?"

How often do we look at the resources God has provided to us, shake our heads, and say, "Not enough"?

But the man who healed the sick, raised the dead, cast out demons, and gave sign after sign after sign that he was quite capable of doing what he said, ignored their excuses and said, "Bring me what you have." He gave thanks to God for the two fish and five loaves and told the disciples to pass out the food.

And everyone ate until they were full.

This is the miracle that Peter and the others witnessed a few hours before the storm: Jesus, taking their meager resources, giving thanks, and then working through those resources to provide more than enough to meet the need.

How often do we turn away from opportunity because we think we are not smart enough, or strong enough, or wise enough? How often do we look at the resources God has provided to us, shake our heads, and say, "Not enough"?

In one respect, we are right. We will never have enough to do God's will—*if we do not have God*. God gives us just enough and asks us to trust him. He says, "Offer your resources to Me, and see what I will do."

It was Peter himself who said not long before he died, "By his divine power, God has given us *everything we need* for living a godly life. We have received all of this by coming to *know him*, the one who called us to himself by means of his marvelous glory and excellence."[12]

Everything we need has already been provided; we receive it when we come to know him. On our own, we can do nothing. But with God, all things are possible. Jesus said that to the disciples; he says that to us.

The Mystery of the Loaves

After the feeding of the 5000, Jesus secluded himself and prayed. The disciples took the boat and began to cross the lake. The storm hit, Jesus appeared, Peter started to walk on the water, Jesus saved Peter, both entered the boat and the storm abated.

And then, Mark's gospel says that the disciples were *astonished* because they did not understand about the loaves and their hearts were hardened. What does this mean, and what does it have to do with Peter?

I think that Peter and the others were astonished because, though they believed Jesus was the Messiah, and that God worked powerfully through him, they did not yet believe Jesus *himself* was God.

They had placed him in a category where other great prophets existed in their minds. People whom God had used in powerful ways but were not themselves God. Yes, they believed he was the Messiah. But they did not yet have a category for God becoming a man.[13]

They had not understood about the loaves because they did not recognize that Jesus had control over all natural forces, including the weather and sea. They had not reflected on the real significance of what Jesus had done when he multiplied the loaves, or raised the dead, or turned the water into wine, because they did not fully understand who he was.

Jesus was not just a servant of God, with a life dedicated to doing God's will. He was also *God himself*, with power to command the forces of nature. If they had understood this, perhaps they would not have been so fearful of the storm, nor so astonished when he calmed it.

Perhaps Peter's own experience as he sank beneath the waves, crying out to Jesus to save him, brought him closer than he had been before to recognizing the true nature of his teacher. Perhaps Jesus' admonition, calling out his "little faith" and asking why he had doubted, propelled Peter nearer to a true understanding of just who it was who had called him.

Whatever it was, we see a change in Peter after this point. A subtle change that will ebb and flow, a growth in understanding that struggles to take root in his impetuous heart. Often we grow the most after we sink to our lowest.

Peter's First Declaration

So what happened after the boat returned to shore? Jesus and the disciples landed at Gennesaret, a fertile area of land near Capernaum on the western shore of the lake. The folks in the area must have been looking for Jesus, because they immediately sent out word that he had been located. Soon, a crowd of people arrived in the area hoping to be healed.

John's gospel goes into great detail about Jesus' teaching that morning. The crowds found him teaching at the synagogue in Capernaum, remembering how he had fed them the day before. Jesus knew their hearts, and told them, "You come to me now because you ate till you were full. Instead of trying to get food that perishes, work for food that lasts for eternal life."

They were intrigued. Food that lasts forever? Yes! But what do we have to do for that food? Jesus' reply is simple and to the point.

"Believe in me."

But their minds were still focused on eating real food. The people who witnessed the multiplication of the bread the day before now asked, "What sign will you give us so that we will believe you? Moses gave our forefathers manna from heaven."

Jesus corrected them. "Uh, that manna actually came from God. God provided the bread. And God is providing you bread from heaven *right now*."

The people grew more excited. Yes, breakfast! "Give us this bread every day," they demanded.

Jesus looked at them with compassion. "*I am the bread that comes down from heaven. If you believe in me, you won't ever be hungry again.*"

Did he just say he was the bread from heaven?

Their confusion and disappointment were obvious. Jesus continued.

"You want a sign? *I am the sign.* You have seen me. Yet you still don't believe."

Now the people began to complain and argue with each other. He promised us breakfast, but now he says he's the bread from heaven! This guy is messing with us—we know his parents! He didn't come from heaven!

"Stop complaining," Jesus said. "I am the bread of life. If you eat this bread by believing in me, you will have eternal life."

John tells us then that many of Jesus' disciples couldn't make sense of what he said. They didn't understand the metaphor. They stopped following him that day and went home.

Then Jesus turned to the Twelve.

"Do you want to leave too?"

It must have been difficult for Peter and the others to listen to their teacher say things that were hard to understand, and then to watch as many turned away. No one wants to be on the losing side. Did they consider it? They were the ones who were closest to Jesus. They witnessed so much of the good he had done. Did they have any doubts, any misgivings, any questions?

It would be understandable if any of the Twelve hesitated before answering. We don't know what the others thought, but Peter spoke up immediately on their behalf.

"Lord, to whom would we go? You have the words of eternal life. We believe and know that you are the Holy One of God."

Peter, who almost drowned during the storm, whose small faith could not sustain him for even a few minutes, who struggled with pride when Jesus asked him to cast his nets out again, this Peter watched as many of the men and women who swore to love and follow Jesus turned away as soon as his teaching didn't comport with their idea of him.

Here is where I see the first sign of real change in Peter. He did not allow his emotion to overwhelm his faith. This Peter is about to have a good day.

"Lord, to whom would we go?"

Who else was there to turn to? John the Baptist was dead and had freely admitted he was not the Messiah. In fact, he was the one who had directed Andrew to Jesus.

The Pharisees and teachers of the law were not trustworthy. Peter had witnessed on more than one occasion how they had tried to trap Jesus and plotted to bring him down.

"You have the words of eternal life."

Though Peter and the others did not always understand everything that their teacher said, they understood enough. And Peter was convinced that Jesus' words pointed the way to eternal life. Jesus had said, "I am the bread from heaven. Whoever eats this bread will have eternal life." Did Peter understand it? Probably not.

But he knew the man.

When we really know someone, we don't have to understand everything. We know their character, we know their heart, and we trust them because we *know* them.

"We believe and know that you are the Holy One of God."

He both *believes* and *knows* that Jesus is God's chosen one. He believes as an act of faith. He chooses to believe and not doubt. Then, from that faith comes knowledge—a conviction that what Jesus said is true, backed by irrefutable evidence that he and the others have witnessed time and time again.

Here the spark of faith ignited in Peter's heart, a spark that will grow over time, but will also be nearly extinguished by coming storms that he does not now anticipate.

Peter's Second Declaration

Peter's confession here was not the only time he declared his belief in Jesus as the Messiah.

After Jesus and the disciples resumed their travels, they made their way to Caesarea-Philippi. As they visited the villages in the area, Jesus pulled his disciples aside and asked them a question. Matthew's gospel provides the most detail about this conversation. Jesus asked them:

"Who do people say the Son of Man is?"

The disciples replied, "Some say John the Baptist; others say Elijah; and still others, Jeremiah or one of the prophets."

"But what about you? Who do *you* say I am?"

Jesus focused on the Twelve. So many others had left, after following him for weeks and months. So many had turned away, forsaking the one they had said they would follow, that they believed in. So many had broken their commitment to be faithful.

He wanted to know about those who were the very closest to him. Was their faith shaken? Did they have doubts? Why were they still here?

"But what about you? Who do you say I am?"

Jesus asks us that question as well. We say we are believers, we say we are committed to following him, but is our commitment only solid when he does what we want him to? When he says what makes sense to us?

Do the doubts rise up when our circumstances are difficult, or when his words are hard to understand? What kind of faith wavers when our emotions are unsettled?

The apostle James describes what we should do when we don't understand: "If any of you lacks wisdom, you should ask God, who gives generously to all without finding fault, and it will be given to you. But when you ask, you must believe and not doubt, because the one who doubts is like a wave of the sea, blown and tossed by the wind. That person should not expect to receive anything from the Lord. Such a person is double-minded and unstable in all they do."[14]

The key is to understand that our faith is not rooted in our circumstances being comfortable, or our understanding being complete. The key is to understand that our faith is in a person, and who we know that person to be.

"Who do you say I am?"

Peter's voice rings out for all to hear.

"You are the Messiah, the Son of the living God."

Once again, Peter's response was the only one recorded. His words strike at the core of our faith.

Who Do You Say I Am?

Our answer to this question will determine the type of faith we actually have. Is Jesus truly God? If so, Scripture says he is trustworthy, in control of all things, good and just, merciful, kind, and forgiving. And if that's the case, why do we worry? Why do we doubt? Why do we struggle when unexpected things happen?

The fact that the question was answered by *Peter* demonstrates the spiritual growth he has undergone in just the few days since the storm. He is becoming more certain of his teacher. His faith is growing stronger. Though he has yet to face (and fail) his biggest test, the time spent with Jesus is slowly changing his heart.

The same happens to us. As we spend time with Jesus, meditate on who he is, talk to him and listen to him through his Word, Jesus slowly changes our hearts as well. Just like Peter.

Jesus was pleased with Peter's words. I imagine a smile coming to Jesus' face, his eyes lighting up at Peter's earnest confession. He replied,

"You are blessed, Simon son of John, because my Father in heaven has revealed this to you. You did not learn this from any human being."

When we believe that Jesus is who he says he is, when we trust him enough to follow him and obey what he tells us to do, we are not only blessed, but the Father himself reveals to us greater spiritual understanding than we had before.

Jesus continues, "Now I say to you that you are Peter (which means 'rock'), and upon this rock I will build my church, and all the powers of hell will not conquer it."

What is he saying?

Is *Peter* the rock on which Christ's church will be built?

Is Peter's *confession* the rock?

Or is Christ the rock?[15]

In the Old Testament, God is repeatedly described as the Rock. Elsewhere in the New Testament, Christ is described as our spiritual rock.[16] Remember, Jesus asked, "Who do you say I am?" It's a question about identity. It's a question about Jesus' very essence. Christ is the rock.

"On this rock I will build my *church*."

What is the church?

The apostle Paul described the church as the "building" made up of believers and built on a foundation that is *Christ*. God lives in the midst of this building. Paul then urged believers not to boast about *human* leaders—naming himself, Apollos, *and Peter*—calling them only servants and co-laborers.[17]

"And all the powers of hell will not conquer it."

What powers of hell?

Sin, death, Satan. All those who call on the name of the Lord Jesus Christ as Savior and God are safe from their power. This blessing is for *us*. Paul reiterates this truth in his letter to the church in Rome:

For I am convinced that neither death nor life, neither angels nor demons, neither the present nor the future, nor any powers, neither height nor depth, nor anything else in all creation, will be able to separate us from the love of God that is in Christ Jesus our Lord.[18]

Then Jesus pronounced a blessing on Peter:

"And I will give you the keys of the Kingdom of Heaven. Whatever you forbid on earth will be forbidden in heaven, and whatever you permit on earth will be permitted in heaven."

To a Jew, these two verses painted a picture of a castle, whose king appointed a steward to be in charge of the keys. The steward had the power to use the keys to open and close doors. As the first disciple to recognize Jesus for who he really was, Peter was blessed with this stewardship.[19]

The keys to the Kingdom refer to the gospel. The message of Christ's death and resurrection is the gateway to the kingdom. Peter was blessed to be the first to open the doors and proclaim the gospel, bringing thousands to faith in Christ.[20] And as we proclaim Christ to those who don't know him, we also participate in God's work, growing His kingdom on the foundation of Christ our king. Peter was the first. We follow in his footsteps.

Yes, it was a very good day.

Personal Reflection

It's easy when we are embarking on a new adventure, to be excited and enthusiastic about the road that lies ahead.

However, as time goes by, what was once a new adventure becomes routine; we begin to take the journey for granted. Particularly when we experience setbacks, it's easy to become weary and forget why we are on the journey, where it is taking us, and who we are following.

As you look at your own spiritual journey with Christ, how have you grown weary or discouraged? What gives you encouragement to keep moving forward?

How can you, like Peter, refocus your attention on the one who is leading you, rather than on your own circumstances or failures?

How would you answer Jesus' question to Peter, "Who do you say I am?"

How does Peter's example of faith encourage you?

For Peter, those few moments of praise from Jesus must have been a great encouragement to him. But even as the sun breaks through the clouds and shines its light on us, it's only a matter of time before the clouds roll in and we must endure another storm. Peter's next storm is already brewing, a storm of his own making, ready to take him down.

---

[12] 2 Pet. 1:3.

[13] Matthew writes that those on the boat worshiped him, saying, "Truly, you are the Son of God." Yet the phrase "Son of God" was interchangeable with the word "Messiah" (See Psalm 2:7). The phrase communicated an especially close relationship—not that the Son of God was actually God in human form.

[14] James 1:5-8.

[15] For an interesting discussion on this passage, see Michael Eisner's book, *The Unseen Realm*, pages 283-286.

[16] 1 Cor. 10:4.

[17] See 1 Cor. 3:1-23.

[18] Rom. 8:38-39.

[19] Later, the other disciples received the same blessing. See Matt. 18:18.

[20] Acts 2:14-41.

My Journal

Chapter 4

The Rebuke

"Jesus turned and said to Peter,

"Get behind me, Satan! You are a stumbling block to me; you do not have in mind the concerns of God, but merely human concerns."

Matthew 16:23

Read First: *Matthew 16:21-27; Mark 8:31-33*

By this point in Peter's journey with Jesus, three Passovers had occurred. The first was after the wedding in Cana when Jesus turned the water into wine. The second was shortly before Jesus appointed the Twelve. The third was around the time of the feeding of the 5000.

Peter and the disciples had been following and learning from Jesus for about two-and-a half years. As we saw in the previous chapter, Peter had come to the point where he could confidently say,

"You are the Messiah, the Son of the living God."

Jesus had praised Peter for this confession, and stated Peter would be given power to declare the kingdom of God to others, ushering thousands into God's presence.[21]

But now, we see Jesus' praise turn to a harsh rebuke: "Get behind me, Satan! You are a stumbling block to me; you do not have in mind the concerns of God, but merely human concerns."

I can only imagine how mortified Peter must have felt in that moment. What happened to bring Peter from the elation of praise to the depths of shame? Let's look at this occasion more closely.

The situation described in these passages occurs soon after Peter's declaration that Jesus is the Messiah. How soon, we don't know. It may have been immediately or it may have been hours (or even days) later, but close enough that Peter was probably still feeling pretty pumped by Jesus' praise.

The gospels tell us that after Peter's acknowledgement that Jesus was the Messiah, Jesus shifted the focus of his teaching. When his miracles were bringing crowds of people to hear his words, he had focused his teaching on the kingdom of God, encouraging people to follow him. But now, he began to emphasize some difficult things that lay ahead.

Jesus knew the time of his death was nearing. Perhaps Peter's confession showed Jesus that the disciples were ready to hear more of what was to come. So now his message to his disciples focused less on how they should live and more on his own coming suffering and death.

It's not like this was the first time Jesus had made allusions to his own death—but that was just the problem—they had been allusions. Prior to this announcement, any mention of his coming death had been veiled in word pictures. It was easy for Peter and the others to miss the point.

For example, during one of their first trips to Jerusalem, when Jesus overturned the money changers tables the first time, some confronted him, demanding to know under whose authority he was acting. Jesus answered, "Destroy this temple, and in three days I will raise it up again." Thinking he meant the actual building before them, they replied, "This temple took forty-six years to build, and you are going to raise it up in three days?"

We know from John's gospel that Jesus was speaking not about the building, but about the temple of his own body. John adds, "After he was raised from the dead, his disciples remembered that He had said this. Then they believed the Scripture and the word that Jesus had spoken."[22]

Another time Jesus foretold of his death and resurrection was when the religious leaders who were plotting to kill Jesus asked him for a sign of his authority. Jesus replied, "A wicked and adulterous generation asks for a sign! But none will be given it except the sign of the prophet Jonah. For as Jonah was three days and three nights in the belly of a huge fish, so the Son of Man will be three days and three nights in the heart of the earth."[23] Again, he foretold of his death, yet his language was so metaphorical that many, including his own students, did not understand.

This time Jesus spoke plainly. Instead of using metaphorical language, he bluntly tells them what's coming next.

He begins with the announcement that he must travel to Jerusalem. This was not unusual. The disciples had traveled with Jesus several times. They had celebrated the Passover with him in the holy city.

In fact, the next Passover was not far off—maybe Jesus was thinking about taking another celebratory trip. Sure, there were risks going to a city where the Pharisees had made it clear that Jesus was not their favorite visitor. But Jesus faced opposition from someone almost everywhere he went.

Their minds probably went to when they would be leaving, how long they would stay, what they should pack....

But Jesus wasn't finished with his announcement. I imagine Jesus raising his hand to stop all the chatter. "Hold on, guys, I wasn't done yet." When they quiet down, he continues, "I must go to Jerusalem." He pauses, making sure he has their undivided attention before he begins again.

"While there, I'm going to suffer. The elders, the chief priests and the teachers of the law are going to hurt me—"

Peter and the others probably looked at each other with alarmed faces. What's he talking about? Does he know something we don't know? They may have gone into defensive mode. They might have begun planning how to protect Jesus. Their faces grow stern. "We can act as bodyguards—we'll take shifts—we will need to bring some weapons. We got this, Master!"

Jesus kept talking.

"Then they will kill me…"

The group was stunned silent.

I can picture Peter shaking his head in disbelief when he hears these words. No way. His thoughts were probably mixed with anger and disbelief. Why was Jesus saying these things? His thoughts were so loud, they must have drowned out Jesus' next few words…

"And on the third day, I will be raised to life."

Perhaps if Peter and the others had not been raised with the image of the Messiah as a conquering hero, they might have remembered that the prophet Isaiah described the coming Messiah as a "suffering servant" who would be "despised and rejected" and "led like a sheep to the slaughter."[24] But Peter's reaction to Jesus tells us Isaiah's description never entered Peter's mind.

A surge of adrenaline likely rushed through Peter. He took Jesus' arm and pulled him aside, out of the direct hearing of the others.

This action raised so many questions for me. Why does he do this? Does he think Jesus has lost his mind? Is he trying to protect Jesus from losing more disciples? Does he believe that Jesus is mistaken or wrong? Does he think that he knows better than Jesus? Does he feel like his relationship with Jesus gives him the right to say, "Uh, dude, lighten up. You're freaking people out with all this crazy talk"?

For whatever reason, Peter acted to put a stop to Jesus' words right away. How could Jesus expect to keep the few disciples he had left if he started talking about being killed!

We don't know what went through Peter's mind, but we know what came out of his mouth.

"Never, Lord! This shall never happen to you!"

And by extension, we know that this statement revealed what was in his heart, for Jesus himself had stated, "Out of the overflow of the heart, the mouth speaks."[25]

The shock Peter must have felt when Jesus then turned to him, looked him in the eye, and spoke with an authority that would silence even the most formidable foe. How each word must have burned as it pierced Peter's heart!

"Get behind me, Satan!"

Now, Jesus was not saying that Peter was actually Satan, but rather, that Peter was speaking words that Satan had actually already said to Jesus during the temptation in the wilderness. Remember when Satan showed Jesus all the kingdoms of the world, saying, "All this I will give to you if you follow me?"[26]

Many believers do not have even the vaguest idea of what the "concerns the God" are. Why? Because they have not engaged the Creator of the universe in so much as a conversation.

Peter was essentially telling Jesus, "You don't need to suffer to fulfill God's will--there's a better way, an easier way," echoing Satan's temptation. Peter was no longer behind Jesus, following him. He had taken his place ahead of Jesus, as one who must guide him.

Jesus replied to Satan then, as he did now to Peter in that moment,

"Get behind me, Satan!"

And now the words aimed directly at Peter...

"You are a stumbling block to me."

How easy it is for us to think we know better than the Lord—that he should listen to us rather than the other way around. But Jesus makes it perfectly clear that the one who takes his place ahead of the Savior is not a leader, but an impediment.

Peter the Rock is now Peter the stone that will trip others up. He has assumed a position that does not belong to him. He has taken on a responsibility that he does not understand and cannot fulfill. He has acted out of an arrogant spirit that says, "I know better than Jesus; I must lead him."

But the words of Jesus bring clarity to the situation. It's not enough to have a strong feeling or even a well-articulated reason when we stray from following Christ. Peter apparently had both feeling and reason. But what is needed is an understanding of the will of God and a willingness to follow no matter what.

The Concerns of God

Jesus next told Peter why he was wrong:

"You do not have in mind the concerns of God, but merely human concerns."

And here is the crux of the matter for both Peter and us. We are primarily motivated by self-interest. We don't naturally have in mind the concerns of God. We have in mind our own concerns. How can *my* life be more comfortable? How can *my* goals be accomplished? How can *I* look good in the eyes of others?

In fact, many believers do not have even the vaguest idea of what the "concerns of God" are. Why? Because they have not engaged the Creator of the universe in so much as a conversation. They do not speak to him in prayer. They do not listen to him by reading his Word. Is it any surprise that they do not know what concerns him?

But Jesus spent daily time with God. He often went off to a solitary place and prayed. He made it a priority to regularly speak with and listen to his heavenly Father.[27]

He also worked hard to communicate to his disciples the concerns of God. He earnestly taught them over and over again what it meant to be a disciple, a follower of God. Soon, he will tell them, "...everything I have learned from my Father I have made known to you."[28] But now, he turned to all the disciples and the crowds that followed them, and said,

"Whoever wants to be my disciple must deny themselves and take up their cross and follow me. For whoever wants to save their life will lose it, but whoever loses their life for me will find it."

And there it is. The hard truth behind being a real disciple. It's not about what *I think I want*. For Jesus, it's about what *he knows I need*. Jesus put us first by laying down his life for each of us so that we can experience real life for eternity. That is what we needed.

He set the pace for us. He blazed the trail that we each must walk. As we follow him, we walk in his footsteps, and live as he lived, "not to be served, but to serve, and to give his life as a ransom for many."[29] We take up our cross. We crucify our old self with its selfish desires, and we fix our eyes on Jesus.

This is what it means to be a disciple. He comes first. We don't second guess. We fall in line behind our commander. We do what he says even when it doesn't satisfy our understanding or make us feel good. Peter will come to know this. He is learning. He still has a lot to learn. Just like us.

Personal Reflection

Do you see yourself in Peter?

Do you ever speak before thinking?

Do you struggle with wanting to be in charge and lead the way?

Do you find yourself interfering in the lives of others because you "know better?"

Do you second guess your leaders, thinking, if they did it my way, it would be more successful?

Do you offer advice without being asked?

I have done all of the above—all, of course, with the best of intentions. But we must learn to stop ourselves and to remember that there is only one who knows all the facts to every situation, who holds the future in his hands, and whose purposes will prevail no matter what.

Years later, near the end of his life, Peter wrote,

Humble yourselves, therefore, under God's mighty hand, so that in due time He may exalt you. Cast all your anxiety on Him, because He cares for you.[30]

I imagine him writing these words, remembering how often his pride brought him down, but that God always lifted him back up again. Perhaps he thought about his own anxious thoughts when Jesus said he would suffer and die, prompting him to arrogantly correct the Son of God. And surely he recalled how Jesus then rebuked him, identifying him with Satan, because he continues,

We must be alert and be on our guard. Be sober-minded and alert. Your adversary the devil prowls around like a roaring lion, seeking someone to devour.[31]

Likewise, we must be alert to the temptations all around us to take the reins in our own hands and be the leader of our own lives. Instead, we must step out of the way, and fall in line, following wholeheartedly, even when the way ahead looks rocky and seems to lead where you don't want to go.

Then the question becomes, are you willing to set aside your own comfort and well-being for the sake of God's kingdom? Are you willing to trust that Jesus knows what is best for your life? Are you ready to truly be his disciple?

Over time, Peter learned to follow. He learned to listen. He learned to humble himself and put others before himself. He messed up in some pretty major ways, but he also persevered. And over time, he changed.

For Peter, things will get worse before they get better. He has yet to have hit rock bottom. That story is still to come.

---

[21] See Acts 2.

[22] John 2:18-21.

[23] Matt. 12:39-40.

[24] See Isa. 52:13-53:12

[25] Matt. 12:34.

[26] Matt. 4:8-9.

[27] See for example Mark 1:35 and Luke 5:16.

[28] John 15:15.

[29] Mark 10:45.

[30] 1 Pet. 5:7-8.

[31] 1 Pet. 5:9.

My Journal

Chapter 5

The Mountain

Peter said to Jesus, "Rabbi, it is good for us to be here. Let us put up three shelters—one for you, one for Moses and one for Elijah."

(He did not know what to say, they were so frightened.)

Mark 9:5

Read First:
Matthew 17:1-9; Mark 9:2-9; Luke 9:28-36; 2 Peter 1:16-18

A few years after my husband and I were married, we saved up to take a 3-week long trip to Europe. We were hoping to start a family soon and figured this would be our last hurrah before having kids.

During our second week, we took an all-day river boat ride on the Rhine River from Koblenz to Mainz in Germany, gawking in awe at the many castles that dotted the cliffs above the riverbanks. We planned to stay that night in a bed and breakfast that had once been the guesthouse of King Ludwig of Bavaria. I was excited!

By the time we had disembarked the boat, picked up our rental car, and ate dinner, it was well past dark. Our bed and breakfast was near the southern border of Germany, so we still had several hours to drive. Once we navigated off the main roadway, we found ourselves driving very cautiously through many circuitous unlit roads to reach our destination.

It was just before midnight when we arrived. It was so dark, we couldn't see six feet in front of us. We were exhausted as the concierge showed us to our room on the second floor. We both sank into the soft feather bed and fell fast asleep.

The next morning I awoke, eager to get a good look at this B&B we had booked sight unseen from across the ocean. After a disappointing housing experience in Paris the week before, I tried to keep my expectations under control. The room was spacious and comfortable, but what about the view? I walked across the room and pulled open the drapes.

My jaw dropped open. My eyes could not believe what they were seeing. Words are inadequate to describe what I saw, though I will try.

The sky was a deep shade of sapphire blue spotted with white puffs of clouds. Punctuating the horizon was a range of huge snow-capped mountains, so clear and sharp that it seemed like I could reach out and touch them. The mountains were reflected below in the bluest lake nestled within a circle of rich green pine trees. And to cap it all off, snow white swans gracefully swam along the lake's shoreline.

It was breathtakingly beautiful, the most awe-inspiring sight I had ever seen. My husband says I screamed. I don't remember anything except thinking, "This is what heaven looks like."

And it is *nothing* compared to what Peter experienced about a week after Jesus' rebuke.

The Radiance of God's Glory

We don't know what happened in that week between the rebuke of Peter and what transpired next, but I imagine the Lord was still trying to get across to his disciples the suffering and death he would experience when they next went to Jerusalem. I can imagine Peter's mood was low. How could he feel otherwise when the man he had followed as Teacher, Rabbi, and Lord was prophesying his own imminent death?

Peter and the others may also have been struggling with their own futures. What would happen to them if Jesus was right? What would they do? Had they wasted the last months and years they had spent following him? If this thought came up, I believe they rejected it quickly. After all, Peter had said, "Lord, to whom would we go? You have the words of eternal life."

Maybe they thought Jesus would perform his greatest miracle and usher in his kingdom with power and glory. More likely, they felt confused and discouraged. Talk about his impending death was not the message they wanted to hear, nor the future they hoped to experience. Perhaps they figured his choice of words was just one more teaching that meant something else, something they were unable to understand just yet.

About a week after the events of the previous chapter, Jesus called Peter, James and John to accompany him on a trip up a high mountain to spend some time praying. They were still in the region of Caesarea-Philippi, so the mountain was most likely Mt. Hermon.

The trip was tiring, and the men were weary when Jesus finally stopped. He then moved a little distance from his disciples and began to pray. The three disciples likely began to pray as well, but Luke's gospel tells us they were soon overcome with sleep. We don't know how much time past before they woke, but what they saw terrified them.

Jesus looked different! His face was changed and radiated like the brightest sun. His clothing glowed with shimmering light. Much later in his life, Peter would recount this moment, saying, "We were eyewitnesses of His majesty. He received honor and glory from God the Father...."[32]

Peter shielded his eyes from the glory he beheld. Then he noticed that Jesus was not alone. Two men were speaking with Jesus. The disciples could hear the words—they were talking about Jesus' coming departure from this world in Jerusalem. Somehow, all three disciples knew that the other two men were Moses, the one who freed the Israelites from Egypt and gave them God's law; and Elijah, the greatest of the prophets who was taken into heaven without experiencing death.

The embodiment of both the Law and the Prophets stood mere feet away speaking to their Lord. Perhaps Peter recalled the words of Jesus when he gave his great sermon on the mount near the beginning of his ministry. He had said, "I have not come to abolish the Law and the Prophets, but to fulfill them."[33]

Now here were the visual representatives of the Law and the Prophets engaged in an intimate conversation with the One who was bringing their work to its rightful fulfillment.

Whether God gave the disciples divine revelation in that moment, or they simply "recognized" those whom they had never seen before, we don't know. But Peter, seeing Moses and Elijah begin to depart, could not help but blurt out to Jesus,

"Lord, it is good for us to be here. If you wish, I will put up three shelters—one for you, one for Moses, and one for Elijah."

Sometimes we react to a moment when we should just wait, experience, and reflect. Those of us who are more comfortable being in charge tend to take the reins as soon as a situation arises that we don't understand or seems unpredictable. We don't like surprises. We like plans. We like results. We prefer action over meditation. We think it's better to do something rather than nothing.

The Man with a Plan

I'm reminded of the account of Martha and her sister Mary. Martha was the one who took charge and had a plan. When Jesus and his disciples stopped by their house for a visit, Martha got busy. So much preparation and cooking to do. She looked for Mary to help her—where was she? Sitting at Jesus' feet listening to him teach.

Martha grew angry, angry enough to demand that Jesus tell Mary to help her in the kitchen. But Jesus turned to her with compassion in his voice, "Martha, you are worried and upset about many things, but only one thing is needed. Mary has chosen what is better, and it will not be taken away from her."[34]

Like Martha, Peter is a person of action. Not only does he suggest building three shelters, but he will also be the one to construct them. He is the man with a plan. He feels useful in this situation. He sees Moses and Elijah begin to depart. He wants them to stay. When Luke wrote his account of this event, he remarked that when Peter spoke, "he did not know what he was saying."

After a week of hearing about suffering and death, it must have been a very welcome shift to Peter's mental state to see Jesus in all his glory alongside Moses and Elijah. Trying to put myself in Peter's sandals, I might have thought, "This is more like it! In fact, how can we make this moment last longer?"

And perhaps that was on Peter's mind also, given that he wanted to build a shelter. The shelter, also called a tent (or tabernacle) was a cloth structure used as a portable sanctuary to house the presence of God. Many centuries earlier, Moses met with God in a tent. God communicated with him face to face while the people remained outside the tent. When Moses came out of the tent to deliver God's message to the people, his face was described as radiant with light.[35]

Peter would have recalled these events from stories told to him as a child. Surely when he saw Jesus, Moses, and Elijah speaking together as they shone with radiant light, he made the connection with Moses speaking to God inside the tent. To be able to recreate that moment now and make it last more than a few minutes would be like heaven on earth. To be present at this time, and bathe in the glory around him would have been far more to his liking than all that talk of suffering and death.

Peter actually wanted to create *three* tents side by side—one for Jesus, one for Moses the Lawgiver, and one for Elijah, the great Prophet—as though all three were on equal footing. He did not comprehend that the work Jesus was doing fulfilled and consumed both the Law and the Prophets.

His desire to build the shelters there on the mountain suggests that Peter pictured Jesus as separate from the people, as Moses had been with the Israelites when he entered the tent to speak with God. Peter did not yet realize that Jesus was God with us, and that all who trust him would have direct access to God through him.

His focus was more immediate and practical: Keep him safe. Keep him separate. Keep him on the mountain. On more than one occasion the disciples had tried to turn people away in order to "protect" their Master. But Jesus often thwarted their efforts. "Come to me, all who are weary and burdened, and I will give you rest," he told the masses.[36]

On another occasion, when they had rebuked some parents for bringing their little children to Jesus, he turned to the disciples, indignant. "Let the little children come to me, and do not hinder them, for the kingdom of God belongs to such as these." He then took the children in his arms and blessed them.[37]

Jesus was God with us, not God set apart and distant.

But impetuous, impulsive, emotional Peter wanted the spiritual high to last, forgetting that Jesus had already told him the days ahead would lead to suffering and death. He had blocked out any thought of Isaiah's prophesies of a suffering Messiah. After all, who wants to dwell on the harshness of life, when glory is radiating right before your eyes?

"Lord, it is good for us to be here. If you wish, I will put up three shelters—one for you, one for Moses, and one for Elijah."

We also see the smallest change in his response to Jesus. He begins his request with, "If you wish." He acknowledges that Jesus is his Lord and his will comes first. Even though Peter doesn't always understand the things Jesus says or does, he is learning to follow. His heart is growing more humble. He is willing to admit he might be wrong.

No sooner were the words out of his mouth, than a bright cloud appeared and surrounded them. Peter, James and John entered the cloud. They were terrified. Their fear only intensified when they heard a thundering voice coming from the cloud. Peter later recounted that moment, "And we ourselves heard this voice from heaven when we were with Him on the holy mountain." God said,

"This is My beloved Son, whom I have chosen. In him I am well pleased. Listen to Him!"[38]

Using almost the exact words said by Moses to the Israelites long ago, God spoke to them directly. God no longer required a human intermediary to stand between him and man. His Son opened the door so that all may have free access to the Lord. The God and Creator of the universe did a marvelous thing here. He spoke to them directly. And what did God say to Peter and the others?

"This is My beloved Son."

Jesus, the man they have followed for two and a half years, whom they believed to be the Messiah, was confirmed by God himself in that moment to be his own Son, begotten by God, clothed in flesh, and dearly loved. When John wrote his gospel, surely he had this moment in mind when he said, "The Word became flesh and made his dwelling among us. We have seen his glory, the glory of the one and only Son, who came from the Father full of grace and truth."[39]

"Whom I have chosen."

Next God proclaimed that He Himself was the One who had chosen Jesus to come into the world to speak God's words to the people. Jesus will tell his disciples in a few days that he "did not speak on [his] own, but the Father who sent me commanded me to say all that I have spoken...So whatever I say is just what the Father has told me to say." The obedience of the Son to the Father was so perfect that Jesus was able to say to his disciples, "The one who looks at me is seeing the one who sent me." [40]

Later, when another disciple asked Jesus, "Lord, show us the Father and that will be enough for us." Jesus answered: "Don't you know me, Philip, even after I have been among you such a long time? Anyone who has seen me has seen the Father. How can you say, 'Show us the Father'?[41]

"In him I am well pleased."

God expressed the pleasure He received from the obedience of the Son. The Father stands solidly behind all that the Son does; He is for Him, because He knows that the Son is fully committed to Him and to doing His will. The Son obeys because He knows that His Father's command "leads to eternal life."[42]

God receives great joy when his children listen to Him and do His will. Jesus gave his Father great joy.

"Listen to Him!"

And here, the command to Peter, James and John is made crystal clear. Especially for Peter, who had disagreed with Jesus' pronouncement of his coming suffering and death, these words from

God Himself were both a rebuke and a command: Stop trying to figure out another path; stop trying to delay what is coming, what must come, what *will* come. Stop closing your eyes and shutting your ears to the one I have sent to you to bring you and all people the opportunity to have real life, abundant life, eternal life. Stop and listen. Listen to my Son. When you listen to him, you are listening to Me.

When God's voice spoke through the cloud, the disciples fell face down in terror. Perhaps the reality of what was really happening was finally setting in. Peter's whole journey with Jesus was not just about following a wise teacher, picking up nuggets of truth, being connected with someone who manifested real power and appeared to be the long-awaited Messiah, the conqueror of oppression, the Savior of the Jewish nation.

No. It was so much more than that.

God's plan was far greater in scope than Peter could possibly have imagined. His picture of Jesus was too small. He had put Jesus in a box of his own defining—a big box, to be sure, but still a box with limitations. Suffering and death fell outside Peter's box. His box will grow much larger in the coming days.

Our Box of Expectations

But don't we do the same thing?

We put Jesus in the box of our own expectations. We say to him, here are the things you can be Lord over in my life. But there are a few things that are off limits. You see, I must feel comfortable with whatever changes you want to bring. I need to give final approval over any detours or U-turns you want to make in my life's journey. If I have a question, we need to stop and you must satisfy my understanding before I can move forward. When you are willing to meet these conditions, I will follow you.

Like Peter, we are weak. We are narrow-minded. We do not (or will not) see the big picture of what God is doing. We struggle with trust, we fear being different, we run from rejection, we hide from hurt. Yet Jesus says to us as he did to Peter and the other disciples, "Whoever wants to be my disciple must deny themselves and take up their cross and follow me."[43]

As Peter, James and John lay shaking on the ground, overcome with terror, Jesus came over and touched them. The voice had stopped. Moses and Elijah were gone. The radiant glow had vanished. It was just Jesus and them once again.

And Jesus, seeing their need, came over and touched them. The Son of God came to them. He reached out his hand and touched them. Because he is God *with us*.

He did not say, "See, I told you so. Now will you listen to me?" He did not expect or demand any special treatment by them. Talk of building three tabernacles was forgotten. No, he saw their need, came to them, and touched them, perhaps a gentle reminder that he was also a man like they were, that they did not need to fear. The moment of glory was just that—a moment. It passed, and now there was work to be done. The Father's work.

"Get up," he said. "Do not be afraid."

Here, too, we hear the Lord speaking to us. The wonder and awe that comes to us when we contemplate the glory of God and all that Christ has done for us must not overwhelm us to the point that we forget the work he has called us to do.

The wonder and awe that comes to us when we contemplate the glory of God and all that Christ has done for us must not overwhelm us to the point that we forget the work he has called us to do.

Whether we give in to fear and lie prostrate on the ground, or we just want to stay on the mountain and worship, Jesus still calls us to complete the mission he began. He does not leave us alone. He did not leave the disciples alone. He is "God with us." He meets us where we are, even if that place is face first in the dirt.

Jesus concludes their trip up the mountain by telling Peter and the others to not tell anyone else about what they had seen until after he had risen from the dead. Why not?

I don't know. Maybe he wanted to prevent people—the other disciples, or the crowds—from focusing on the wrong thing. Maybe he wanted to circumvent the possibility that others would erect three tents in the hopes of another appearance. Maybe because their minds might be filled with images of glory rather than images of suffering.

Maybe because he knew the pivotal moment in the course of history would not happen on this mountain, but very soon on a much smaller hill at Golgotha, outside the city walls of Jerusalem. He wanted them focused on what really mattered.

Personal Reflection

Peter kept what happened on that mountain a secret, though in his heart he surely relived that moment over and over again. After Jesus was crucified, resurrected and ascended into heaven, Peter recalled what happened on the mountain. Before a crowd in Jerusalem, he preached the fulfillment of a prophecy made thousands of years earlier:

"For Moses said, 'The Lord your God will raise up for you a prophet like me from among your brothers. You must listen to Him in everything He tells you.'"[44]

From originally seeing that moment as an opportunity to bask in the glory of Christ, staying on the mountain, building tents for the Jesus, Moses, and Elijah, to later seeing that moment as an opportunity to share the good news of what Jesus had done to a crowd of unbelievers, Peter's heart had changed. His vision had grown.

By then, Peter understood so much more than he did on the mountain. As the days draw nearer to their arrival in Jerusalem for the Passover, Peter will continue to face extraordinary challenges that will chip away at his self-assuredness and pride.

What challenges do you face as you try to follow Christ?

How has this account of Peter's experience on the mountain connected with you?

Do you like to take charge of situations in order to meet your own agenda?

Do you prefer to "stay on the mountain" and bask in the glory of the Lord?

Have you put Jesus in a box of your own expectations, holding him hostage until he does life your way?

Or perhaps your fear keeps you from following Christ, as you take up your cross?

"This is My beloved Son, whom I have chosen. In him I am well pleased. Listen to Him!"

How will you respond to God's words?

---

[32] 2 Pet. 1:16, 17.
[33] Matt. 5:17.
[34] Luke 10:42.
[35] Exo. 34:34-35.
[36] Matt. 11:28.
[37] Mark 10:13-16.
[38] 2 Pet. 1:18.
[39] John 1:14.
[40] John 12:44-50.
[41] John 14:8, 9.
[42] John 12:50.
[43] Matt. 16:24.
[44] Acts 3:22; See Deut. 18:15.

My Journal

Chapter 6
The Cost

*"Look," said Peter, "We have left everything to follow You.
What will there be then for us?"*

Matthew 19:27

Read First:
Matthew 19:16-30; Mark 10:17-31; Luke 18:28-30

The day after the transfiguration on the mountain in Caesarea-Philippi, Peter, James and John followed Jesus down to join the other disciples. They began traveling south, crossing the upper Jordan River into Galilee, heading towards their home base in Capernaum. Along the way, Jesus took time to minister to the crowds of people that came to him, healing their sick.

Suddenly, the father of a demon-possessed boy knelt before Jesus, pleading for mercy for his son who had seizures that endangered his life. Apparently, the father had brought the boy to the disciples while Jesus was away, but they were unable to heal the boy. Jesus cast out the demon, healing the boy.

The disciples asked Jesus why they had been unable to heal the boy. Jesus spoke plainly: "Because you have so little faith. Truly I tell you, if you have faith as small as a mustard seed, you can say to this mountain, 'Move from here to there,' and it will move. Nothing will be impossible for you."[45]

The disciples had been operating out of their own strength, rather than putting their faith in him. It was imperative that they understood that without him, they could do nothing.

Jesus then returned to the topic that his disciples did not want to hear—another prediction of his impending death in Jerusalem. He told them, "The Son of Man is going to be delivered into the hands of men. They will kill him, and on the third day he will be raised to life."[46]

When they heard his words, Peter, along with all the disciples, were again filled with grief. They did not understand what he meant, and they were afraid to ask him.[47]

As they moved closer to Capernaum, they also moved closer to Jerusalem. I think about what must have been going through Peter's mind during the walk, and the emotions he had to have been experiencing.

To see what he saw on the mountain would have been incredibly encouraging—scary, yes—but also encouraging, because it more than confirmed everything he longed for and believed. Jesus was truly the Messiah!

How he must have longed to share his experience with the others, to assure them especially now, when they struggled with Jesus' words and a foreboding sense of doom. But Jesus had told them not to speak a word of what had happened until after his death.

Making sense of his death was not something Peter knew how to do. How would dying solve anything? Would it restore Israel to its rightful position as a sovereign nation under God? Would it cause the armies of Rome to retreat across the Mediterranean? Every step he took closer to Jerusalem filled him with dread. How could *death* lead to *victory*?

If something happened to Jesus, what would become of their group? Jesus had only been gone overnight, and the disciples were already floundering when they tried to heal. They were not ready; they were not trained enough. They needed Jesus. They couldn't do anything without him.

If Jesus really did die, what would they do? What would Peter do? Was it all for nothing? He couldn't accept the possibility of this last thought—so many had been healed, so many believed that Jesus was the Messiah, so many left families and homes to follow him. Surely, some greater plan or purpose existed that he simply was not yet seeing. He clung to the hope that all would soon make sense.

The Folly of Self-Promotion

After a couple of days of traveling, they arrived home to Capernaum. But tensions among the disciples were high. They had argued on the road. Some thought that Jesus' death would usher in the kingdom of God. If so, would Jesus be handing out positions of leadership to them? They began to compare themselves to each other—who was the greatest? Who would receive the highest honors? Who would be recognized and favored?

I can hear them as they touted their merits: "I'm Jesus' favorite!" "Well, I was the first to be called!" "Yeah, well, Jesus called me the Rock!" "I've got you beat—Jesus told me that I would see heaven open and the angels coming and going, whatever that means." "I was there when Jairus' daughter was raised to life—you weren't!" "Jesus took me on the mountain with him!" "Well, I walked on water—at least for a minute." And so it went on and on. When Jesus asked them what they were arguing about, they kept quiet.

But Jesus knew their hearts. He knew what battles raged in their minds, what temptations the enemy whispered in their ears. He sat down among them, waited until he had their undivided attention, and said quietly, "Anyone who wants to be first must be the very last, and the servant of all."

He then gestured to a little child in the room. Taking him in his arms, he continued. "Do you see this child? Whoever welcomes this little child in my name welcomes me; and whoever welcomes me welcomes the one who sent me. For it is the one who is least among you all who is the greatest."[48]

They stared at Jesus with blank expressions. Did they understand? Did they grasp what he was saying? Did they see that status and position and power meant *nothing*? That serving and humility meant *everything*?

We all want to be number one. We want to be first. We want to be the best. If we are not the best, we try to find a way to get there, whether through determined effort, manipulation, or downright malice.

Apparently not, because shortly after his talk with them, as soon as the following day, they came to Jesus and proudly told him they had stopped a man from casting out demons in Jesus' name because he was "not one of us," as though being a disciple of Jesus gave them special privileges or status.

Jesus simply told them, "Don't stop him. Whoever is not against us is for us."[49] Over and over he taught his closest followers what it really meant to be a disciple.

I'm reminded of an incident that occurred with the students of John the Baptist shortly after Jesus began his ministry. They had noticed that many of the people who used to follow the Baptizer were now following Jesus. They complained to John, "Uh, excuse me, Teacher, but that man you told us about—he's now baptizing people—and everyone is going to *him!*"

John listened patiently to their complaint before saying, "Listen, you all knew I was not the Messiah. I made that very clear. I told you my role was simply to point people his way. I have done what God told me to do, and that fills me with joy."

Their worries about being overshadowed by Jesus were put to rest when John stated quite plainly,

"He must become greater; I must become less."[50]

It's easy for us to see success as meaning being more popular or having more friends than others do. If you are on social media, you know that getting "likes" or growing your followers consumes many people. We tend to compare ourselves with those around us and then feel either envious of them if we think they have more, or proud of ourselves if we judge ourselves as having the upper hand.

We all want to be number one. We want to be first. We want to be the best. If we are not the best, we try to find a way to get there, whether through determined effort, manipulation, or downright malice.

Jesus' disciples had missed the big picture of what was most important—that God's kingdom was proclaimed, that people were turning to God, that God's will was being accomplished. They needed to let go of *self*-promotion and begin *God*-promotion. But they continued to be plagued by concerns for their own futures and their own security as they continued toward Jerusalem.

The Cost of Following Jesus

All along the journey, Jesus taught and healed. Large crowds followed him. Luke's gospel tells us that the crowds of people on the road numbered in the thousands.[51] Whenever they stopped, people surrounded Jesus. They came to be healed and to learn.

And they kept on bringing their little children to Jesus for him to bless. Jesus did not turn them away. He underscored the importance not of power or position or popularity, but of humility and innocence. The children had no ulterior motives in coming to Jesus. He was not a means to an end for them. They came to him freely without demands or expectations. Jesus tried to explain to his disciples,

"Truly, I tell you, anyone who will not receive the kingdom of God like a little child will never enter it."[52]

What did the disciples think about Jesus' words? What did he mean when he said anyone who will not receive the kingdom of God like a little child will never enter it? What did Peter think? We have a bit of a clue based on what happened next.

After Jesus blessed the children, he got up and began to walk away. A young man ran to him, kneeling before him. The gospels described him as a ruler and very wealthy. He looked up at Jesus and said, "Good Teacher, what must I do to inherit eternal life?"

Jesus answered his question with another question.

"Why are you asking me about what is good? Only God is good."

Jesus drew attention to the man's use of the word "good." Who does this young man really think Jesus is? If God alone is good, then the man is acknowledging that Jesus is God. If Jesus is God, the man should believe and obey whatever Jesus says.

If, however, his use of the word "good" was just a polite term, and he viewed Jesus simply as a prophet or esteemed teacher, then he would be obligated to seek eternal life in the manner already set up by God—by keeping all the commandments of God perfectly.

Peter and the disciples paid close attention to their Teacher's answer to the young man.

Jesus told him, "If you want eternal life, keep the commandments—do not murder, do not commit adultery, do not steal, do not lie, do not cheat others, honor your father and mother, and love your neighbor as yourself."

The man responded, "I've kept all the commandments since I was a boy. What else do I need to do?"

Jesus looked at the young man with love in his eyes and told him what he saw within the man's own heart. "There is one thing missing from your life. If you want to be perfect, sell everything you own and give to the poor. Then you will have treasure in heaven. Then, you can follow me."

Now, the real answer to the question, "Who do you think I am?" will be given by the young man. If he believes Jesus is God, he will obey what Jesus said, sell his possessions, give to the poor, and follow Jesus.

But if he does not believe Jesus is God, he has nothing to fall back on but his own righteousness. His only path forward is perfect obedience to the commandments, a task that none but a *perfect* man would be able to accomplish.

And this is why the man walked away in sorrow. His great wealth became the stumbling block on the only path to eternal life.

As the man departed, Jesus turned to his disciples, "I tell you the truth, it is hard for a rich man to enter the kingdom of heaven. In fact, it's easier for a camel to pass through the eye of a needle than it is for a wealthy man to enter God's kingdom."

The disciples were astonished. If a rich man can't make it into heaven, what hope was there for anyone else?

"Who then can be saved?" They said to one another.

Jesus answered. "With man, this is impossible. But with God all things are possible."

What's In It for Me?

Peter took all this in. He had always thought those who were wealthy had it so much easier than those in his own station of life. When times were hard, and you struggled to put food in the mouths of others, you didn't have the luxury of focusing on the spiritual side of life—you had to work.

Those who did not have jobs because of personal wealth had the time and energy to follow all the rules that the religious leaders taught. They were able to give large offerings and spend time reading the Torah. Surely, they had an advantage when it came to the question of inheriting eternal life? They inherited everything else—why not eternal life?

Yet his Teacher was saying it was hard for a rich man to enter God's kingdom. If it was hard for *them*, it must be *impossible* for us! He began to consider the past couple of years and all he and the others had given up to follow Jesus. He then asked the question that surely was on the minds of the other disciples as well.

"What about us? We have left *everything* to follow you. What then will there be for *us*?"

Peter's question may have been largely economic. After all, he was a businessman before giving up his livelihood to follow Jesus. Was his investment in Jesus worth it? How much more did Jesus expect from them? Would the rewards outweigh the costs?

Peter's mindset shifted away from Jesus and his work, to Peter and *his* work. Just as the wealthy young man wanted to know what work he needed to do to inherit the reward of eternal life, Peter wondered what reward he would receive for the work he had already invested.

His question reveals his heart. *What's in it for me?*

Here, once again, I feel that familiar tug on my own heart as I think about times when I contemplated the same thing. What's in it for me? Will I receive a good return for the time and energy I'm being asked to invest? The Bible clearly teaches that each will receive according to what they have done—but it sure sounds like that reward isn't given until we reach heaven.

But what about now? What's the benefit *now*?

For Peter and the other disciples, their own welfare was never far from their thoughts. They clearly visualized the sacrifices each of them had already made, while failing to recognize the sacrifice that their Lord repeatedly told them was coming for him.

They probably compared themselves to the young man—unlike him, they had left everything for Jesus. So what would they get in return? What reward, or honor, or place of power would they receive for their sacrifice?

Jesus did not chastise Peter for his words. Though the disciples' focus was on their own immediate concerns, Jesus knew that he was speaking with men who were both fallible and weak. He did not belittle or downplay what they have given up.

He told them that their sacrifice was not unnoticed. He assured them that anyone who had sacrificed for the sake of following him would receive in this lifetime a hundred times what was lost. When the time came for him to sit on his throne in heaven, they would also receive eternal life. Perhaps this response satisfied Peter and the others for a time, but as we shall see in the next chapter, the thought of reaping eternal rewards in the here and now lingered at the front of their minds.

Peter and the other disciples had been following Jesus for two and a half years. Most would spend the rest of their lives taking up their cross daily to follow him and fulfill the great work he would give them to do. And the cost to follow him would multiply exponentially.

Were they in it to the end, through good times as well as bad, until God called them home? Or was their gaze more settled on immediate gratification for what they had already given up?

Jesus added, "Many who are first will be last, and the last will be first."

It's not as though Jesus was less than forthcoming about what he expected from them. He had been very up front, especially on this final trip to Jerusalem.

To the large crowds who traveled with him, Jesus had said, "Any one of you who does not give up everything he has cannot be my disciple" (Luke 14:33).

To the man who said, "I'll follow you but I have family business to take care of first," Jesus had said, "No one who puts his hand to the plow and then looks back is fit for the kingdom of God" (Luke 9:61-62).

To the scribe who swore, "I'll follow you wherever you go," Jesus had replied, "Foxes have dens and birds of the air have nests, but the Son of Man has no place to lay His head" (Matt. 8:19-20).

To the follower who said, "Let me wait until my father is dead and buried," Jesus had responded, "Follow Me, and let the dead bury their own dead" (Matt. 8:21-22).

To the wealthy young ruler, who asked, "What must I do to inherit eternal life?" Jesus had answered, "Sell everything you own and give to the poor. Then you will have treasure in heaven. Then, follow me."

To his disciples, Jesus had clearly stated,

"Anyone who loves his father or mother more than Me is not worthy of Me; anyone who loves his son or daughter more than Me is not worthy of Me; and anyone who does not take up his cross and follow Me is not worthy of Me" (Matt. 10:37-38).

To *everyone*, Jesus says,

If anyone wants to come after Me, he must deny himself and take up his cross and follow Me. For whoever wants to save his life will lose it, but whoever loses his life for My sake and for the gospel will save it (Mark 8:34-35).

Following Jesus comes with a cost. How willing are we to count that cost? How willing are we to keep looking forward, pressing on toward the prize, forgetting what is behind, to follow Jesus?

Peter is still learning about cost. When the cost seems too high, he will face his greatest failure.

Personal Reflection

Do you tend to view your life like a bank statement that must be balanced? All credits and debits must be accounted for. All debts must be paid. It's a happy day when the balance works out in our favor. How can this kind of mentality work against you wholeheartedly following Christ as Lord and Savior?

Or are you more concerned with your social standing? Is your success measured in followers, friends, and likes? Do you feel good when others "heart" your posts, or take the initiative with you, or say nice things about you? How can this kind of mentality work against you wholeheartedly following Christ as Lord and Savior?

How do you feel about being last? How do you feel about being a servant? How do you feel about sacrifice? Jesus may not ask you to sell all you have and give to the poor—that may not be the obstacle in *your* heart. But what obstacle *does* block you from wholeheartedly following Christ?

How do you feel about taking up your cross—your instrument of death—and carrying it every day? Do you, like Peter, want some sort of reassurance that God has your back? Will you really be satisfied with the reward he has promised?

Or do you ask, "What's in it for me?"

---

[45] Matt. 17:20.

[46] Matt. 17:22.

[47] Matt. 27:22-23; see also Mark 9:30-32.

[48] Luke 9:48.

[49] Mark 9:39.

[50] John 3:30.

[51] Luke 12:1.

[52] Mark 10:13-16.

My Journal

Chapter 7

The Refusal

"Lord, are you going to wash my feet?"

Jesus replied, "You do not realize now what I am doing, but later you will understand." "No," said Peter, "you shall never wash my feet."

John 13:6-9

Read First: *John 13:1-17*

What a week it had been! After traveling for weeks on end, Jesus, Peter and the other disciples arrived a short distance from Jerusalem, across the Jordan River, where John the Baptist had preached repentance and baptized so many.

While there, Jesus received word that his dear friend Lazarus was gravely ill at his home in Bethany.

Jesus delayed visiting his friend for two days. Then he told his disciples to head for Bethany. They tried to dissuade Jesus from going there. "Teacher, don't you remember not that long ago the Jews there tried to stone you?" Peter and the other disciples must have feared for his life, for Thomas told the rest, "Let us also go, that we may die with him."[53]

When Jesus finally arrived at Lazarus' home, Lazarus had been dead four days, long enough for the body to have begun decaying. Jesus called for Lazarus' tomb to be opened. Surely the thought that Jesus would raise Lazarus from the dead was on Peter's mind. After all, this was not the first time Peter had seen Jesus bring someone back to life.

The first time was when he raised the 12-year-old daughter of Jairus, a synagogue leader back in Galilee. But she had only been dead a short time when Jesus raised her.[54]

The second time had occurred during their recent travels. As they had passed through Nain, a small village in lower Galilee, they had come across a funeral procession for the only son of a widow. Since Jewish funerals typically happened the day following a death, this young man would only have been dead for a day. The joy his mother experienced at receiving her son back alive was a sight Peter would not forget![55]

Now, Lazarus. Dead four days. In the tomb for three. Even his grieving sisters hesitated at the idea of opening the tomb. His decaying body would carry with it a strong odor. But they obeyed their Lord and instructed the servants to move the stone that sealed the tomb. In the presence of many witnesses, Jesus commanded Lazarus to come out of the tomb.

And just like that, Lazarus obeyed his Lord and rose from the dead, still wrapped in his burial cloths!

What an amazing confirmation that must have been to the faith of Peter and the disciples. This man, who was able to raise even the dead by the command of his voice, was without doubt the Messiah.

Many believed in Jesus after witnessing this miracle. But others rushed the two miles to Jerusalem to tell the Pharisees what had happened. A council was convened that same day, and the religious leaders began plotting how to take Jesus' life.

Who was Jesus, Really?

Jesus and the disciples kept a low profile, staying away from Jerusalem for the time, withdrawing to a little village called Ephraim, about 17 miles away from the city. How long they remained there is not certain, maybe only a few days. During their stay, Jesus healed the sick and taught quite a bit on what the end would look like.

Six days before the Passover, on a Saturday, Jesus and the disciples walked back to Bethany to the home of Lazarus and his sisters. A dinner was given in Jesus' honor that night.

I wonder how on edge Peter might have been feeling. After all, Jesus kept speaking about leaving, about suffering, about dying. But Peter would also still have fresh in his mind the power demonstrated by the raising of Lazarus. He would still remember his time with Jesus on the mountain, when Moses and Elijah appeared with him. He would still be replaying that thundering voice from heaven, calling Jesus his beloved Son and commanding Peter to listen to him.

How he longed to go back there and forget Jerusalem!

Now, at Bethany, their group was scarcely a half hour walk from Jerusalem, where powerful people plotted to kill Jesus. Was Peter on alert, watchful and ready to protect his Lord at any moment?

Events during the dinner that night didn't assuage Peter's anxiety in the least. When Mary, Lazarus' sister, began to pour priceless perfume on Jesus' feet, wiping them with her hair, Judas reprimanded her, saying, "Why wasn't this perfume sold and the money given to the poor?" Not that he actually cared about the poor. He cared more about the money.

Jesus put a stop to Judas' rebuke with words that pierced Peter's own heart. "Leave her alone," Jesus replied. "It was intended that she should save this perfume for the day of my burial. You will always have the poor among you, but you will not always have me."[56]

Burial? What burial? Here then was just one more reminder of an end that Peter was trying his best to avoid thinking about. On top of that, he learned that now the religious leaders were also plotting to kill Lazarus.

"You will not always have me."

Jesus had alluded to this several times lately. What did he mean? Where was he going? Was someone planning to take him somewhere? As large crowds of people arrived at the house to see both Jesus and Lazarus, Peter didn't know who to trust. Any one of these people could be spies from Jerusalem, or worse.

Did Peter get any sleep that night? I think I would be tossing and turning, reliving all the great moments that pointed to a triumphant Messiah and Savior, while trying to shut out the whispers of a suffering, dying Servant.

Who was Jesus, really? What had he come to do? Who had he, Peter, committed to follow?

That following morning was Sunday. Preparations were made for their entry into Jerusalem. When Jesus asked two of the disciples to run ahead and borrow a donkey for the journey, the reference to the Old Testament prophecy was not lost on Peter: "Rejoice greatly, Daughter Zion! Shout, Daughter Jerusalem! See, your king comes to you, righteous and victorious, lowly and riding on a donkey, on a colt, the foal of a donkey."[57]

Rejoice!

King.

Righteous.

Victorious.

These were words you could cling to and hope in. Yet there was also that word "lowly." He didn't want to think about *that* word, but then another memory forced its way into his thoughts.

While traveling here, shortly after encountering the rich young man, Jesus had broken up a disagreement between the brothers, James and John, and the rest of the disciples. The brothers, along with their mother, had asked Jesus to allow them to sit at his right and left when he came in all his glory. The others had heard and grown indignant.

Peter had joined the other disciples in their outrage at James and John. Perhaps he and the others believed they had more right to those seats of honor than the brothers did. Perhaps they were just upset that they hadn't thought of asking first.

But Jesus shut down the discussion when he said to them all, "You know that the rulers in this world flaunt their authority over those under them. *But you will not be like that.* If you want to be a leader over others, you must first be a *servant,* and whoever wants to be first before any other, must be the *slave* of everyone else. For even the Son of Man came not to be served but to serve others and to give his life as a ransom for many."[58]

Peter pushed that memory back out of his mind. He refused to see his Teacher as anything other than the conquering Messiah his people longed for and expected. And his time on the mountain and the voice that spoke proved that Jesus was the one they had all been waiting for.

He was the long-expected Messiah, their "Wonderful Counselor, Mighty God, Everlasting Father, Prince of Peace." His lips formed the rest of Isaiah's prophesy, written hundreds of years earlier, "Of the greatness of his government and peace there will be no end. He will reign on David's throne and over his kingdom, establishing and upholding it with justice and righteousness from that time on and forever."[59]

Yes, Jesus was the fulfillment of the ages, the conquering hero, and the salvation of Israel. That thought warmed Peter's heart and energized his spirit. Danger lay ahead, but Peter was ready to fight for his Lord.

Triumphant King? Or Humble Servant?

As they approached Jerusalem and entered through the city gates, they were welcomed by praise and shouts of joy from the crowds. The people laid their cloaks and palm branches at the feet of the donkey on which Jesus rode, hailing their king, their Messiah. Both before and behind him, they welcomed Jesus, crying out,

"Hosanna to the Son of David!"

"Blessed is He who comes in the name of the Lord!"

"Hosanna in the highest!"[60]

Peter was delighted with the welcome, though he remained alert to any hint of trouble. Their triumphant entry into the city only reinforced his confidence that Jesus would usher in the kingdom of God with power and glory. Whatever those who opposed Jesus tried to do, Peter was ready to respond swiftly.

When Jesus then entered the temple courts and began overturning the tables of the money changers, Peter likely took his actions as a precursor to replacing the oppressive Roman government, as well as the corrupt teachings of the religious leaders, with the righteous kingdom of God. Even though rumors of his imminent arrest circulated among the people, Jesus returned that night to Bethany, only to return on the following three days, teaching the people.

Thursday evening arrived. Peter and the other disciples entered the upper room of a house located in the city for their Passover celebration. They sat down to eat when Jesus got up from the meal, removed his outer garment, and wrapped a towel around his waist. The disciples watched in silence. They weren't sure what was happening. Was Jesus illustrating a new parable before them?

Then Jesus poured water in a basin and knelt before the disciple closest to him. He gently took each dusty foot of the disciple and washed it clean, drying it with the towel around his waist. Surely the disciples looked at each other with confusion in their eyes. What was Jesus doing? It was the job of the servants to wash their feet—not their Master.

For a moment, no one spoke.

Then Jesus reached Peter, kneeling before him. Peter recoiled. "Lord, are you going to wash my feet?" He asked with incredulity. Peter was horrified. Surely, Jesus did not mean to act like a servant. It had been a long week. He must be overtired and didn't understand what he was doing, Peter rationalized.

Jesus knew Peter was confused. He tried to calm Peter's reaction by saying, "You do not realize now what I am doing, but later you will understand." Peter was the one who lacked understanding, not Jesus. But Peter thought he had to correct Jesus once again. It didn't go well when he tried that earlier; it won't go well now either.

The disciples often failed to understand what Jesus did or said, but many times he clarified his words and actions after the fact. But Peter wasn't having it. This activity flew in the face of everything Peter was hoping for. A king does not serve! How quickly he had forgotten Jesus' words while on the road from Galilee, "Even the Son of Man came not to be served, but to serve."

"No," said Peter, "you shall never wash my feet."

"Never" is a strong word to use against Jesus. Though Peter probably meant well, he failed to recognize that obedience to his Teacher was required not only when Peter thoroughly understood what the Teacher meant, but especially when he did not. It's easy to follow someone who is doing what you would do anyway; it's much harder to follow when we disagree or don't understand. That's when trust must come in.

When Peter said, "Never," Jesus made his position very clear: "Unless I wash you, you have no part with me."

Jesus' words are rich with meaning. Here, he assumes the duties of a servant, humbly lowering himself from his rightful position in order to show his followers what real love looks like. The verses that begin this account say, "Jesus knew that the hour had come for him to leave this world and go to the Father. Having loved his own who were in the world, he loved them to the end."

This act of service he performed for his disciples was an act of love, one that he expected them to emulate with each other. By this act he tells Peter and the rest, "Stop thinking about gaining glory or power through positions of authority. Stop arguing about 'who is the greatest' or who will sit at my right and left hand. Consider others better than yourselves. Serve one another; love one another—as I have loved you, love one another. If you will not, you are *not* my disciple."

"Unless I wash you, you have no part with me."

These words of Jesus also have a deeper spiritual meaning. Washing removed dirt. By washing the disciples' feet, Jesus also demonstrated the spiritual cleansing he brought to them. He symbolically represented his ability to forgive and remove sin—not through a display of attention-grabbing power, but through a choice to lower himself from King of kings to humble servant. As a servant, he came to bring spiritual cleansing to all people. By refusing to allow Jesus to wash his feet, Peter would exclude himself from the very mission Jesus came to fulfill.

I'm reminded of the words written by the apostle Paul many years later. He described this attitude that Jesus adopted when he wrote:

"...being in very nature God, [he] did not consider equality with God something to be grasped, but took the very nature of a servant, being found made in human likeness. And being found in appearance as a man, he humbled himself and became obedient to death—even death on a cross!"[61]

"Unless I wash you, you have no part with me."

Would Peter set aside his ambition, his personal security, his need to control, his vision for the future, his hopes, his desires, his ideas of what should and shouldn't be, and *simply obey*? Would he realize that his refusal to be washed, though having the appearance of humility, was actually his own pride repulsed by the idea of a Savior who was also a Servant?

It should come as no surprise that Peter reacted dramatically to Jesus' words, making a complete about face:

"Then, Lord," Peter replied, "not just my feet but my hands and my head as well!"

A few minutes earlier, Peter had told Jesus "No," that washing his feet was too much. Now, he tells Jesus he's not doing enough. Control is a hard thing to let go of. But he is trying. He knows he wants to be a part of whatever Jesus is doing. So, if Jesus wants to wash him, why not wash all of him?

How often do we call Jesus our Lord, yet refuse to actually submit to him? We don't understand, or we don't want to, or we are too busy, or we are afraid, or we might look bad in the eyes of others. The list of excuses seems unending.

Kind, patient Jesus answers Peter. "Those who have had a bath need only to wash their feet; their whole body is clean. And you are clean..."

Those who are followers of Jesus have had the bath already. But that doesn't make us perfect. We must still come to the Lord to have the dust of living in this fallen world washed from our feet.

We don't stop sinning when we commit our lives to Jesus. The sinful nature will be with us until he returns and exchanges our earthly bodies for one that is incorruptible and eternal. There is a reason Jesus said to take up our cross daily. It is a daily choice to say no to the temptations all around us and die to self.

But Jesus wasn't only focused on each individual and their need for washing. No, there was more to come.

When he was done washing the last pair of feet, he put on his clothes and sat down among them. Now was the time to make this experience clear for them, for Peter. He asked them all, "Do you understand what I have done for you?"

Remember when Jesus told Peter, "You do not realize now what I am doing, but later you will understand"? Now was the later he spoke of. I'm sure the disciples were confused, but by now they were used to having Jesus' words and actions explained to them. They listened attentively. I imagine Peter especially locked in on Jesus, since he was the one who the Teacher had once again corrected. Jesus continued speaking.

"You call me 'Teacher' and 'Lord,' and rightly so, for that is what I am. Now that I, your Lord and Teacher, have washed your feet, you also should wash one another's feet. I have set you an example that you should do as I have done for you."

Peter had called him Lord just moments earlier when he questioned Jesus' act of service. "Lord, are you going to wash my feet? ...No, you shall never wash my feet!" How often do we call Jesus our Lord, yet refuse to actually submit to him? We don't understand, or we don't want to, or we are too busy, or we are afraid, or we might look bad in the eyes of others. The list of excuses seems unending.

But Jesus is making another point here. He said, "I have set you an *example* that you should do as I have done for you." The forgiveness and grace and love he extends to each of us, we must extend to one another. We must wash one another's feet. We must humble ourselves. We must serve one another. We must forgive each other. We must love one another. We must treat others as better than ourselves.

He tells this to Peter. He tells this to the disciples.

He tells this to us.

Jesus continues. And it almost seems like he is speaking directly to Peter in light of what just happened between them. He says, "Very truly I tell you, no servant is greater than his master, nor is a messenger greater than the one who sent him." Does Peter feel the gentle correction? Does he realize that he had tried twice to tell Jesus what not to do, and then what to do?

"You shall never wash me!"

"Wash not only my feet, but my whole body as well!"

As a final encouragement to them, Jesus concludes, "Now that you know these things, you will be blessed if you do them." He wants them to be blessed, to experience the good that the Lord has for all who do his will. But there is a difference between knowing what we should do and actually doing it. Knowledge alone does not bring blessing. Obedience brings blessing.

This all took place on Thursday evening. He spends these last precious moments at dinner with his disciples to show them what it really means to follow him. After dinner, he and the disciples will walk to a garden where Jesus will pray. He knows he will be betrayed, arrested, abandoned, beaten, whipped, and crucified in the next few hours. He knows that his followers will scatter and fear for their lives.

But he also knows the story doesn't end there. It's just the beginning.

Personal Reflection

Imagine going on a hike on a hot summer day. Imagine peeling off your shoes and socks. Your feet are probably smelly and sweaty. Now imagine that the person you most respect, the person who want to impress, the person you esteem more than any other takes your stinky sweaty feet in their hands to clean them.

I think I would freak out. I would respond exactly like Peter did. "No way! You are not going to get anywhere near my feet, much less clean them!" I would be embarrassed and horrified. What will they think of me now that they know the condition of my feet?

Jesus knows something even *more* disgusting. Jesus knows the condition of our *hearts*. He knows the sin that lurks in the shadowy corners. He knows all our dirty little secrets. He knows the malicious thoughts we hide behind a smile. He is not surprised. He is not shocked. He is the one who said, "It is not the healthy who need a doctor, but the sick. I have not come to call the righteous, but sinners, to repentance."[62]

How are you like Peter?

Is there an area of your life which you are unwilling to allow the Lord to "clean"?

Are you trying to "understand" before you are willing to obey?

Are you willing to humble yourself and serve others?

Is there an area of control that you need to surrender to him?

This night with Jesus is far from over for Peter and the disciples. The next few hours will take Peter to probably the very lowest point in his life. He will be forced to face the truth about himself and be utterly broken by what he finds.

The "Rock" will hit rock bottom.

---

[53] Read the account of Lazarus, John 11:1-16.

[54] Read the account of Jairus' daughter, Mark 5:21-43.

[55] Read the account of the widow's son, Luke 11:7-17.

[56] John 12:7.

[57] Zech. 9:9.

[58] Matt. 20:20-28; Mark 10:42-45.

[59] Isa. 9:6-6.

[60] Matt. 21:9; Mark 11:9-10; John 12:13.

[61] Phil. 2:6-8.

[62] Luke 5:31-32.

My Journal

Chapter 8

The Vow

Peter replied, "Even if all fall away on account of you, I never will."

"Truly I tell you," Jesus answered, "this very night, before the rooster crows, you will deny me three times."

But Peter declared, "Even if I have to die with you, I will never disown you."

Matthew 26:33-35

Read First:

Matthew 26:31-35; Mark 14:27-31; Luke 22:31-34; John 13:33-38

That dinner weighed heavily on Peter's mind. Once again, he had allowed his mouth to move faster than his brain. Why couldn't he learn to wait and listen, instead of making a fool of himself? Sometimes, it felt like he was outside his own body, watching himself dig one hole after another and then fall into it, and he didn't know how to stop.

Once again, he had tried to take control of the situation and act like he himself was the teacher, and Jesus was the student.

When Jesus said that unless Peter allowed Jesus to wash his feet, he could have no part of him, Peter had tried to fix things. But then he had swung way too far in the opposite direction, once again telling the Master what to do. "Wash my head and hands too, while you're at it!"

Peter could kick himself. Why am I always making a fool of myself? Why can't I do what Jesus wants the first time? Why do I always stick my foot in my mouth?

Years later, the apostle Paul described this very problem in his (and our) lives. "I do not understand what I do. For what I want to do I do not do, but what I hate I do...I do not do the good I want to do, but the evil I do not want to do—this I keep on doing."[63]

Haven't we all been there at some point in our lives? We mean to say *one thing*, but *another* comes out of our mouths. We hear ourselves, and think, "Whoa, that's not what I meant to say, but I can't admit that now. I'll look foolish." And so we push forward, making a bigger and bigger mess.

Part of the problem is, we don't know what we are saying. We haven't taken the time to think it through and choose our words carefully. We just haphazardly open that foolish hole in our faces and let go, come what may. Then we are surprised that our words were not exactly what we intended.

I imagine that when Peter saw Jesus approaching him to wash his feet, he meant to say, "Lord, you are God, I am just a sinful man. I am not worthy of you to touch my feet, let alone wash them." If he had *really* thought it through, that is.

But instead, his words were wrapped in an attitude of "I know better than you in this moment. You obviously have a huge misunderstanding about our roles—you are Lord, and I am your student. This is not how a Lord acts. But I can help you with that. Just do what I say."

"You will never wash my feet!"

Peter had a second opportunity at that point. Jesus tried to help him through the moment, saying, "You do not realize now what I am doing, but later you will understand." Right then, Peter had an "out." He could have responded, "You're right, Lord. I don't understand what all this means. But I do know that whatever you say or do is right, and I will submit to you."

Instead, he said, "Never!"

We are so like Peter. We jump to conclusions. We misread situations. We rely on our own understanding. We blurt. We contradict ourselves. We always think we know better.

After realizing the consequences of his obstinacy, he abandoned his original position and was ready essentially to take a shower, once again failing to submit to Jesus' desire and intent.

We are so like Peter. We jump to conclusions. We misread situations. We rely on our own understanding. We blurt. We contradict ourselves. We always think we know better.

We fail to trust the one to whom we owe our very existence, as though he is somehow not enough.

We should not be surprised by our own stubborn, willful, doubting, prideful, and foolish behavior. Jesus isn't. In fact, he had plenty to say on the topic. Over the course of the three years of his ministry, he used some hard but truthful words to his disciples, some of which we have already looked at:

"Why are you so fearful? How is it you have no faith?"

"You of little faith. Why did you doubt?"

"You have so little faith! Why are you arguing with each other about having no bread? Do you still not understand?"

"Get behind me, Satan!" he said. "You do not have in mind the concerns of God, but merely human concerns."

"O unbelieving generation, how long must I be with you? How long must I put up with you?"[64]

These are words that could just as easily be spoken to us today. But before we feel down or discouraged, we must remember that Jesus also knows our hearts and the nature of our flesh, and he exemplifies the love and compassion of God the Father toward us all:

"For he knows how weak we are; he remembers we are only dust."

"The spirit is willing, but the flesh is weak."

"Father, forgive them, for they don't know what they are doing."[65]

As I read about Peter's experiences during the dinner, I feel a surge of compassion for him. I know what's coming. I've read ahead. I know that this evening, tomorrow, and the next day are going to be the worst days of his life. He will see the darkest corners of his own heart; and he will watch himself do things he swore he would never do.

The Passover Meal

After the dinner was finished, Peter joined in singing psalms with the other disciples and Jesus, as was customary at the end of the Passover meal.

Peter reflected on the meal itself. The Lord seemed strangely introspective, changing the usual pattern of celebrating the Passover meal. Typically, certain recitations were made during the course of the meal, reminding the participants about their ancestors' bondage in Egypt, their deliverance by God through Moses, and the fateful and deadly night before their exodus from Egypt took place.

The Passover was a significant Jewish holiday which commemorated the Exodus story, telling how the Israelites were freed from slavery in Egypt under the leadership of Moses. The journey would eventually bring them to the land promised by God to their forefathers. This night Jesus made a few unexpected and alarming statements during the eating of the meal.

Part of the meal was eating unleavened bread, or bread made without yeast. Yeast often symbolized sin in the Jewish faith. Traditionally, eating the unleavened bread reminded people of the haste with which they left Egypt—they left so fast there was no time to let the dough rise—hence the bread was unleavened.

The disciples watched as Jesus took the bread, broke it, and made a new declaration: "This bread is my body which is broken for you. Whenever you eat it, remember me and what I have done for you."

And then Jesus took the cup of wine, which represented the blood of the lamb that marked the doorframes of God's people in Egypt. Anyone whose doorframe was marked with the blood of a spotless lamb would be saved from the angel of death who "passed over" that night. To this ritual, Jesus added, "This wine is the new covenant in my blood, which is poured out for you."[66] By drinking the wine, they were to remember how he, the spotless lamb of God, had poured out his blood to save them from death.

While Peter was mulling over this new teaching, Jesus continued with an announcement that stunned all the disciples so much, that talk about the bread and wine was set aside. Jesus announced that one of them in the room was going to betray him! Poor Peter, now he had to worry about that as well!

Peter didn't understand. Betrayal by one of the twelve, his body broken for them, and his blood poured out for them—along with all his ominous predictions of suffering and death in Jerusalem--Peter must have felt overwhelmed and confused. Surely Jesus would take the time to explain his meaning to them.

Final Warnings

After dinner was wrapped up, they left the room and began walking outside the city walls toward the Mount of Olives. Judas left the group and headed deeper into the city, presumably on some errand for Jesus. As the rest walked, Jesus made another cryptic statement. "My children, I will be with you only a little while longer. Where I am going, you cannot come."

Peter paused, hoping Jesus would follow-up with some sort of clarifying statement. Instead, he said, "A new commandment I give you: Love one another. As I have loved you, you also must love one another. Then everyone will know that you are my disciples, if you love one another."

In his haste to ask his next question, Peter barely paid attention to Jesus' words. "Wait, Lord, where are you going?"

Jesus replied, "Where I am going, you cannot follow now, but you will follow later."

Not good enough. Peter needed details, blurting out, "Lord, why can't I follow you now? I will lay down my life for you."

Then Jesus paused, looked Peter in the eyes and asked, "Will you really lay down your life for me?"

Peter stared at Jesus, for once at a loss for words. His thoughts raced. How can Jesus question my loyalty? How can he doubt my devotion to him? Have I not spent the past three years following him around the countryside, leaving everything behind, putting my own life at risk? Was I not the one who first declared that he was the Christ?" Thoughts of his own "accomplishments" crowded out the times he had failed Jesus and been rebuked.

Jesus stopped and looked at Peter with compassion. He spoke to him with gentleness and love, but also with a cautionary tone. "Simon, Simon, Satan has asked to sift you as wheat."

The first thing Peter noticed was Jesus called him Simon, and not Peter. The name brought back his former life, his time as a boy, his work fishing all night long, hoping for a good catch. *That* Simon had a different goal for his life. *That* Simon had not yet met the Lord. *That* Simon had not yet been called to leave everything behind and follow Jesus. Did Jesus now see him as that same man?

Perhaps Peter realized in that moment that he indeed was still that man. Every time he tried to control Jesus, or failed to listen to his Lord, or missed the entire point of a teaching, he was Simon. Peter was the name of the man who followed his Lord faithfully. Peter was the new man; Simon was the old man. Yet both lived within him.

"Satan has asked to sift you as wheat."

Peter painfully recalled the time when Jesus had rebuked him, calling him Satan, telling him he was an obstacle to the ministry of Jesus. That had hurt deeply. This statement, now, frightened Peter. What did it mean to be sifted as wheat?

Peter knew the process of sifting wheat. The grains were shaken and roughly agitated in a sieve until the good parts separated from the chaff or bad parts, which were then disposed of. Was Satan testing him? Was he trying to break him? If that's what Satan was up to, Peter would not give him the satisfaction. Yet even as his indignation overcame the fear in his heart, Jesus' next words floored him.

"But I have prayed for you, Simon, that your faith may not fail. And when you have turned back--"

Turned back? Did he say, *turned back*? That implies first turning away. Did Jesus really think that Peter would turn away from him, leave him, abandon him?

"And when you have turned back, strengthen your brothers."

The end of that last sentence was lost in the turmoil that resulted from Jesus' next words.

Jesus turned to include the other disciples. "This very night you will all fall away on account of me, for it is written: 'I will strike the shepherd, and the sheep of the flock will be scattered.' But after I have risen, I will go ahead of you into Galilee."

Peter thought maybe the others might leave, but he would never leave. He only thought about himself in that moment, even though Jesus had just told him to strengthen his brothers. They only entered his mind as an example of what he would *never* do.

He loudly declared his intent with determination and resolve. "Even if all fall away on account of you, I never will. I am ready to go with you to prison and to death!"

Jesus tried once more to reach his obstinate follower. Jesus gazed deeply into Peter's eyes. "Look at me, Peter. I am telling you the truth. Today—yes, this very night—before the rooster crows, you will disown me three times."

Here then was the challenge. Before everyone, Jesus had put Peter's reputation on the line. This was the way he could finally prove to his Master that he was worthy, that he was faithful, that he was more than willing to follow him to the very end. Peter insisted emphatically, "Even if I have to die with you, I will never disown you."

The walk was interrupted by claims of faithfulness from the other disciples as they continued traveling toward the Mount of Olives. Jesus led the way to a little olive grove in a garden at Gethsemane. The place was not unknown to the group—they frequently used this spot for prayer or meditation.

Now, the thoughts of all weighed heavily on the words Jesus had spoken. Not only was there a traitor among their midst, but now Jesus had said that all of them would fall away, abandoning him.

Peter's mind was anguished but determined to do whatever it took to prove himself faithful. Even so, he struggled with what he had heard. Jesus was leaving them, going somewhere they couldn't follow. He would be betrayed by one, abandoned by the rest, and that Peter himself would deny him not once, but three times.

His mind reasoned, this must be some kind of metaphor—something that Jesus would explain in the morning. Peter just couldn't deal with it now. He was so tired, not so much from physical exertion, but from mental and emotional exhaustion. He needed to sleep, but they also still needed to pray. And Judas had still not returned from his errand. They would probably wait for him before turning in for the night.

The one thing he didn't think about was Jesus' very last words before predicting Peter's denial. He always seemed to be missing the tail end of Jesus' teachings. He did not remember until much later that Jesus had also said, "After I have risen, I will go ahead of you into Galilee."

This was not the first time Jesus spoke not only of dying, but of rising from the dead. Even those who *opposed* him remembered him saying he would rise again after three days.[67]

If Peter had paid attention and listened, perhaps he would have dealt better with all that was about to happen in the next few hours and days. But his mind was too preoccupied with other things. He would remember later.

The good news was that the story was not over. Betrayal, suffering and death would not have the final word. Another chapter was yet to come.

Peter would see Jesus again. But right now, he was being "sifted." And the turbulence he was experiencing was about to reach fever pitch.

Personal Reflection

Impulsive. Controlling. Prideful. Stubborn. Unteachable.

A lot of chaff needed to be sifted out of Peter's heart. But he is not unique. In fact, he's pretty typical. We all have chaff in our hearts.

Thankfully, we have a God who doesn't see our sin and disgustedly walk away. We have a God who sees our heart, knows our darkest secrets, realizes we are mere dust, and loves us with a love that knows no bounds. He says to his people, "I have loved you with an everlasting love," so that we can say, "How great is the love the Father has lavished on us, that we should be called children of God! And that is what we are!"[68]

What chaff still lies in your heart?

Do you find yourself, like Peter, putting your foot in your mouth too many times?

Do you, like Peter, step outside of your own circle of responsibility and try to control the people and situations around you?

Do you, like Peter, fail to listen to all that the Lord is saying, preferring to pick and choose what you will hear and what you will not?

Do you, like Peter, compare yourself with others, and feel like you have to prove that you are worthy of God's love?

How did God speak to you through Peter's struggles on this night?

The night is not yet over. Satan will sift Peter heartlessly, yet Jesus' words are true in the midst of the struggle. "I have prayed for you that your faith may not fail." And he prays for each of us this very day:

Christ Jesus who died--more than that, who was raised to life--is at the right hand of God and is also interceding for us.... Therefore he is able to save completely those who come to God through him, because he always lives to intercede for them.[69]

Peter had the Lord right there with him. He could reach out his hand and touch him. Though Jesus is not physically with us, we still have complete access to him at all times. "Let us, then, approach his throne with confidence, that we may receive mercy and find grace to help us in our time of need."[70]

He didn't fail Peter, as we will see. He won't fail us either.

---

[63] Rom. 7:15, 19.

[64] See Matt. 8:26, 14:31, 16:8-9; Mark 8:33, 9:19.
[65] See Ps. 103:14; Mark 14:38; Luke 23:34.
[66] Luke 22:19-20. See also 1 Cor. 11:23-26.
[67] Matt. 27:63.
[68] Jer. 31:3; 1 John 3:1.
[69] Rom. 8:34; Heb. 7:25.
[70] Heb. 4:16.

My Journal

Chapter 9

The Garden

"Simon, are you asleep? Why are you sleeping? Couldn't you keep watch with me for one hour?" he asked Peter.

"Get up! Watch and pray that you will not enter into temptation."

Mark 14:37; Matthew 26:40

Read First:
Matthew 26:36-46; Mark 14:32-42; Luke 22:39-46

None of the gospel accounts of the time spent in the Garden of Gethsemane record Peter (or any of the disciples), saying anything while Jesus was praying. But Jesus himself had things to say *to* Peter that give us a little more insight into the man himself.

The Garden of Gethsemane was located outside of Jerusalem's city walls at the foot of the Mount of Olives. At one point, it contained a grove of olive trees with a working olive press. While the original garden passed away with time, a few very old olive trees still grow in the area, reminiscent of the time when Jesus took refuge among them.

As Jesus and the disciples approached the gate in the still of the night, the garden sat quiet and serene. It had become a place of retreat for Jesus where he would sit and meditate or pray to his Father. It would now be the place where he came for strength to face both the physical and spiritual agony that was only hours away. Luke's gospel tells us that on this particular week, Jesus and the disciples spent their nights on the Mount of Olives after teaching at the temple during the day.[71]

After they entered the garden gate, Jesus directed his disciples to wait at the entrance, while he took Peter, James, and John farther into the garden to pray. Peter could see that Jesus was very troubled and distressed, but he didn't know what to say or do. His mind replayed bits and pieces of the events of the evening: betrayal, denial, suffering, death. He felt helpless, overcome with both sorrow and exhaustion.

Jesus turned to his three closest disciples and said, "My soul is overwhelmed with sorrow and anguish, to the point that I feel like I am at the edge of death. Stay here and keep watch with me."

The gospels do not record a response from Peter, James or John, but I imagine they assured Jesus that they would do as he asked, keeping watch for any signs of danger. What else could they say?

Jesus then moved further into the garden, far enough away for privacy, but not so far that they could not keep him in their sights or hear snatches of his prayers in the quiet of the night.

Jesus' Prayer

Peter watched as Jesus stopped "a stone's throw" or about 50 feet away. Instead of standing to pray, as was usual for the time, Jesus first fell to his knees, overwhelmed with the reality of what lay before him in the coming hours. Peter strained his eyes to see the kneeling figure of his Lord in the shadows of the olive trees. He watched as Jesus then lowered his upper body so that he lay face down on the ground in a posture of utter anguish. Then Jesus began to pray.

Though Jesus may have begun praying quietly, over the course of his time in the garden, his prayers grew more distressed and vocal, offering up "prayers and petitions with fervent cries and tears to the one who could save him from death."[72] Later, Peter recounted to Mark the parts of the prayer that he was able to hear. Jesus prayed,

"Abba, Father..."

Jesus' use of the word "Abba" to address his heavenly Father only occurs once, here in the gospels. "Abba" was a very personal and intimate name used by a beloved child for their daddy or papa. Imagine a small child, hurting and afraid, turning to their daddy to help them, to rescue them from danger. Jesus cried out to his "daddy" in his greatest hour of need, saying,

"All things are possible for you."

Peter heard Jesus repeat these words that he had so often told Peter and the others. As recently as when they traveled from Capernaum to Jerusalem on this latest and last trip, he had spoken of God's all-powerful nature. Peter remembered the rich young ruler who had sorrowfully turned away from following

Jesus. He had been astonished when Jesus said how hard it was for the wealthy to enter the kingdom of heaven. If even the wealthy, with all their money and power, could not enter the kingdom, how, then, could *anyone* hope to enter? But Jesus broadened their perspective when he said, "With God, all things are possible."

With this statement uttered now in the garden, Jesus recognized the reality of his current situation. Yes, God can do anything. We can always turn to him and ask for his help. We can approach God's throne of grace with confidence and ask for mercy in our time of need.[73] Nothing is impossible for him. But sometimes, the greatest good is only accomplished through sacrifice and hardship.

Sometimes, God says *no*.

"If you are willing, take this cup from me."

Here Jesus asked his Father to allow him to walk a different path, to drink another cup, but only after recognizing that God's *willingness* to act takes priority. Jesus does not ask God to do anything that is not in line with God's plan to restore the relationship between God and man that was broken so many years ago in another Garden.

"Yet not what I will, but what you will."

Again, Jesus subjugated his will to that of his heavenly Father. He is fully committed to following his Father's will. It is the only path he wants to take.

The Weakness of the Body

If Peter had still been alert enough to pay attention to Jesus' prayer, his next few days may have been easier to bear than they ended up being. But at some point about now, Peter succumbed to the weariness and sorrow that weighed him down. He fell asleep, a brief escape from the stress of the day.

After about an hour of praying, Jesus rose and found Peter, James and John all fast asleep. But Jesus singled out *Peter*.

"Simon, are you asleep?"

I imagine Peter struggling to wake himself up as Jesus continued,

"Why are you sleeping?"

How does one answer that question?

I was tired?

It's been a crazy week and an even crazier night—it's all been just too much to deal with.

Because my comfort is more important to me at this minute than doing what you asked of me.

It was just forty winks—I wasn't completely asleep!

We all have so many excuses when we don't do the thing Jesus asks of us. Perhaps Peter doesn't offer an excuse in this moment because he knows that only a few hours earlier he swore, "Even if all fall away on account of you, *I never will*—I am ready to go with you *to prison and to death!*"?

He's ready for prison and death, but *not* ready to give up his sleep. Jesus is clearly frustrated at the weakness he sees in his top three followers. He asked Peter,

"Couldn't you men keep watch with me for even *one hour*?"

Peter alone is addressed, though all three were guilty of falling asleep rather than keeping watch. Why address only Peter?

Maybe because Peter was so outspoken about his own righteousness, his own ability to do more and do better than anyone else, that he needed to recognize the weakness within him. He had yet to learn that his strength, his power, his ability to choose right and resist wrong was solely dependent on his reliance on Jesus.

Or maybe because Jesus saw the potential in Peter to be a leader to the others, to encourage and strengthen them, to be an example to them of someone who wholly puts his trust in the Lord?

Just as Jesus submitted himself to his Father's will and "learned obedience from what he suffered," Peter would also learn humility by what he would suffer in the coming days.[74]

A few hours earlier Peter swore, "Even if all fall away on account of you, I never will—I am ready to go with you to prison and to death!"? He's ready for prison and death, but not ready to give up his sleep.

Jesus continued, "Get up."

The first admonition is actually quite practical. "Get up." It's harder to fall asleep if you are upright.

My husband and I sometimes watch a little television before going to bed at night. There's always a point where my body moves from vertical to horizontal on the couch. We both know when this happens that I will be asleep within minutes. But somehow I keep sabotaging my own efforts to stay awake.

Occasionally, the solution to warding off sleep is not that difficult. We just need to stay upright.

Now, I realize Peter's situation was not anything like my own. The emotional strain of the evening, coupled with all the mental confusion and physical exertion, had taken its toll. He literally was exhausted, as were James and John.

But when your leader asks you to watch and pray, you should actually do your best to watch and pray. Jesus understood this. On this first "break" from his praying, Jesus repeats what he said to the disciples upon entering the garden, but this time, adding the *reason* for staying alert:

"Watch and pray so that you will not enter into temptation."

Jesus knew what was coming. He knew that his followers, and especially Peter, needed to be alert and ready. He knew that each of them was being sifted like wheat by the enemy and needed to remain alert to the schemes of the devil.

Much later, Peter will repeat the essence of Jesus' words in his first letter to the churches: "Be alert and of sober mind. Your enemy the devil prowls around like a roaring lion looking for someone to devour. Resist him, standing firm in the faith, because you know that the family of believers throughout the world is undergoing the same kind of sufferings."[75]

Peter learned through his own failure the importance of obedience. He, like Jesus, had learned obedience through what he suffered.

"The spirit is willing, but the body is weak."

Jesus finishes his admonition with a note of empathy to Peter's situation. He himself endured pain and suffering in his body to fully obey his Father's will. He knew the weakness of the body. He experienced it in the garden. He would experience more the following day.

His physical, emotional, and mental suffering was foretold about 700 years before he came to earth by the prophet Isaiah:

He was despised and rejected—a man of sorrows, acquainted with deepest grief. We turned our backs on him and looked the other way. He was despised, and we did not care... He was pierced for our rebellion, crushed for our sins. He was beaten so we could be whole. He was whipped so we could be healed... the Lord laid on him the sins of us all.[76]

Jesus understood suffering. He understood the temptation that comes with suffering. The writer of Hebrews tells us that

Jesus is able "to empathize with our weaknesses" because he had "been tempted in every way, just as we are." Because he "suffered when he was tempted, he is able to help those who are being tempted."[77]

He was fully aware of the suffering he would endure when he prayed to his Father, "Yet not my will, but your will be done." He would not allow the weakness of his own body stand in the way of fulfilling God's purposes.

With that, Jesus turned back into the garden, continuing to pray, "My Father, if it is not possible for this cup to be taken away unless I drink it, may your will be done."

We don't know how long this second prayer time lasted, but when he returned to the three, he *again* found them sleeping.

The gospel writers do not tell us what Jesus said this second time, but we do know that he said *something*, because all three were speechless and "did not know how to answer him." Most likely, he repeated the question he asked at first, "Why are you sleeping?"

It's hard to imagine Peter without anything to say. Clearly portrayed in the gospels as the most verbose of the disciples, often blurting without thinking first, to be at a loss for words indicates a bit about his state of mind. I think it's safe to say that at this point Peter felt like a failure. He had let his Lord down. All his words of bravado during the supper earlier that evening, all his boasting of his own uprightness and superiority compared to what the other disciples might do, may have been ringing in his ears about now.

After Jesus returned to prayer for the third time, perhaps Peter gave a valiant effort to try to wake himself. Maybe he stretched his limbs and did a few jumping jacks in an effort to get his blood flowing, but any efforts on his part were short-lived. When Jesus returned the third time, Peter was again asleep.

The spirit is willing, but the flesh is weak.

We have some reason to wonder, however, if Peter did stay awake for at least a little while as Jesus prayed. Mark's gospel, for which Peter is a source witness, tells his audience something that the other three do not. Mark relates that as Jesus prayed, an angel from heaven appeared to him in the garden and strengthened Jesus. Mark goes on to say that Jesus' anguished prayer became more earnest until his sweat looked like drops of blood falling to the ground.

Was this account something Peter witnessed and told Mark about later? Or did Peter learn from the risen Lord about the angel's visitation? Again, we don't know. We do know that Jesus returned to the disciples for the third time, saying,

"Are you still sleeping and resting? Enough! Look, the hour has come, and the Son of Man is betrayed into the hands of sinners. Rise! Let us go! Here comes my betrayer!"

Personal Reflection

Have you ever gone through a difficult time in your life when trouble seemed to follow you at every turn? Have you ever felt like you were so emotionally or physically exhausted that you could not take one more step or make one more decision?

The "sifting as wheat" has begun in Peter's life. He is being forced to recognize his own physical, spiritual, and mental limitations. Like Peter, we must learn that we are helpless without the Lord. We cannot continue to trust in our own abilities rather than in him. The man who boasted of his own steadfast devotion to the Lord is getting a glimpse in the mirror at his own frailties and weaknesses. The test has only just begun.

How have you trusted in your own abilities rather than trusting in Jesus? How have you allowed the weakness of your own body excuse your responsibility to the Lord?

I can think of times in my life when I've been given an opportunity to serve someone, and I just didn't want to do it. I was too tired. Or I was short on time. Or I had better things to do. My excuses were all "me-centered." If God is presenting the opportunity, he will also provide the strength to carry it through.

It's work. It's hard. But we are not alone. Many have gone before us, including Peter, *and* we have a great example to follow:

Therefore, since we are surrounded by such a great cloud of witnesses, let us throw off everything that hinders and the sin that so easily entangles. And let us run with perseverance the race marked out for us, fixing our eyes on Jesus, the pioneer and perfecter of faith. For the joy set before him he endured the cross, scorning its shame, and sat down at the right hand of the throne of God. Consider him who endured such opposition from sinners, so that you will not grow weary and lose heart.[78]

It's easy to grow weary and lose heart, to give up when trouble comes. It's easy to fix our eyes, not on Jesus, but on our own strength, our own abilities, our own understanding or our own ideas of how things should be.

Times will come when, like Peter, we will fail to stay alert, fail to watch, fail to pray, fail to endure. But Jesus knows us. He knows that we are dust. He knows that even though the spirit may be willing, the flesh is weak. And that is why he intercedes for us, he gives us his Holy Spirit to help and comfort us, he promises to always be with us.

How did this account of Peter's time in the garden resonate with you? How are you like Peter?

71 Luke 21:37.

72 Heb. 5:7.

73 Heb. 4:16.

74 Heb. 5:8.

75 1 Pet. 5:8-9.

76 Isa. 53:3-6.

77 Heb. 4:15; 2:18.

78 Heb. 12:2-4.

My Journal

Chapter 10

The Impulse

Simon Peter reached for his sword, drew it out and struck the servant of the high priest, cutting off his right ear.

But Jesus answered, "No more of this!" And he touched the man's ear and healed him.

Jesus commanded Peter, "Put your sword away! Shall I not drink the cup the Father has given me?"

Luke 22:49; John 18:10-11

Read First:

Matthew 26:47-56; Mark 14:44-50; Luke 22:47-51; John 18:2-11

"Are you still sleeping and resting? Enough! Look, the hour has come, and the Son of Man is betrayed into the hands of sinners. Rise! Let us go! Here comes my betrayer!"

The firm and resolute voice of Jesus pierced the ragged rest of Peter. That moment he was thrust from the relative safety of sleep into a reality he had refused to accept would be part of his future. Now, that future fractured the idealism with which he had insulated himself for so long. Peter awoke to the nightmare he had feared and dreaded, though Jesus himself had prepared and warned him about what was coming many times again.

A surge of adrenaline rushed through Peter's body as he jumped up to face whatever unseen danger approached them in the darkness. He could hear the rhythmic march of soldiers, the stern clipped orders of a commanding officer, the softer yet more sinister murmur of voices growing closer as he stumbled after Jesus toward the garden gate. The other disciples followed behind them, still groggy yet making every effort to present a united front to whatever threatening force approached them from beyond the gate.

The first person Peter saw was Judas.

He remembered Judas had left their group during dinner the night before. Judas knew the location of the garden—he had been with them on many other occasions when Jesus came here to pray or spend the night. Was he only now just returning? What had he been doing these past few hours?

Directly behind Judas, Peter was alarmed to see a large detachment of Roman soldiers and temple guards, as well as some officials from the chief priests and the Pharisees. After them, a menacing crowd of men trailed, armed with swords and clubs, carrying torches and lanterns to light their way.

Peter likely didn't know what to think. Had Judas been arrested? He did not look like he was bound in any way. It appeared like he was guiding the group to Jesus. But why? It was still the middle of the night. Why was Judas here, now, with these people?

Peter's mind would not yet consider the terrible possibility that Judas had done the unthinkable.

The Kiss of Betrayal

Peter was caught off-guard as Judas alone approached Jesus. Moving closer to kiss him, Judas called out to Jesus, "Greetings, Rabbi!" Jesus responded, momentarily putting the greeting on pause.

"Judas, are you betraying the Son of Man with a kiss?"

When Peter heard these words, the full realization of their meaning stunned him. Was Judas the one Jesus spoke of last night during supper? Was Judas the traitor? He shook his head in utter disbelief.

I wonder if Judas hesitated for the briefest of moments when he heard Jesus' words, or was he fully determined to carry through the act that would define him as the greatest villain of history? Whether he felt anything at Jesus' words or not, he proceeded to kiss the man he swore to follow, thereby confirming the identity of the one the soldiers had come to arrest. In one act of feigned affection, Judas condemned his Master to death.

The kiss was not a symbol of any form of devotion for his Master, but rather served as a sign of betrayal. After the kiss, Jesus clearly unmasked both Judas' hypocrisy and evil intent for all to hear. "Friend, for what a purpose you have come!"

Jesus knew what Judas was doing. He was fully aware of Judas' heart and thoughts. He did not express any surprise or dismay at Judas' actions. He accepted his fate. Even though it came from the hands of one of his own disciples, Jesus knew that ultimately this was the path his Father had chosen for him. That knowledge brought him both peace of mind and focused resolve to carry out the will and purposes of his Father.

Judas then returned to the large crowd that waited to arrest Jesus. Peter's eyes followed Judas. Confusion, anger, disbelief, and outrage all swirled within his mind. Peter was utterly shocked by what was transpiring; he couldn't fully wrap his head around the events happening before him.

Jesus, however, knew exactly what was happening. He stepped confidently toward the soldiers and asked them, "Who is it you want?"

"Jesus of Nazareth," they replied.

"I am," Jesus said. Not "I am he" as some translations record, but simply "I am," the two little words that God himself used when Moses asked what he should tell Israelites when they ask for his God's name. "I AM," the Almighty responded.

With this declaration, John's gospel tells us the crowd drew back and fell to the ground.

Why? We are not told. Perhaps some in the crowd had seen Jesus perform miracles and only then realized this was the man they were seizing.

Maybe his time in the garden, praying to the Father, and being strengthened by an angel, left him in a state where the glory of the Lord within him could not be contained, spilling out before the eyes of many witnesses.

Or possibly his statement that he was "I AM" overwhelmed the Jews in the crowd with the recognition that God himself stood before them, strong, calm, and in control.

Peter saw the impact on the crowd. His thoughts raced wildly without direction or control. Was this the time his Master would take his stand in power and glory and usher in the Kingdom? Running on pure adrenaline, Peter's hand moved instinctively to the hilt of his sword.

Again, Jesus asked the soldiers, "Who is it you want?"

"Jesus of Nazareth," they again replied, though this time from their crouched position on the ground.

Jesus answered, "I told you that I am he. If you are looking for me, then let *these* men go." It is not surprising that Jesus' first concern was not for himself, but for the safety of the eleven men who walked with him, learned from him, and would go on to suffer for him for the rest of their lives.

Then the soldiers stepped forward and seized Jesus to arrest him. This act of aggression against their Lord immediately prompted the disciples to action. As they rallied to their Master's side, they asked, "Lord, should we strike with our swords?"

Peter did not wait for an answer. He was ready for a fight, to prove himself loyal, to fulfill his declaration before Jesus and all the other disciples that he was willing to die for Jesus.

The servant of the high priest, a man named Malchus, stood nearby, watching the soldiers carry out their instructions. Peter drew his sword and swiftly moved toward the servant. With a quick flick of his blade, Peter sliced off Malchus' right ear. The man yelped with pain as the blood coursed down the side of his face, and he fell to his knees.

Jesus immediately put a stop to the violence. "No more of this!" he told Peter. With the same compassion he had shown to so many suffering people during his three-year ministry, Jesus reached down and touched the servant's wound. His ear was completely healed.

Jesus then turned his attention to Peter. In a voice of stern authority, he commanded Peter, "Put your sword away! Shall I not drink the cup the Father has given me? For all who draw the sword will die by the sword."

Who Was This Man?

Peter stood there, stunned. Were they supposed to just allow their Lord to be arrested? What was expected of them? His need for understanding superseded the knowledge he already had—that Jesus had only ever asked them to trust him and obey.

"Shall I not drink the cup the Father has given me?"

The word "cup" echoed in Peter's mind. Flashes of moments spent with Jesus rapidly created a collage of images and emotions within him.

To James and John, he had said, "Can you drink the cup I am going to drink?"

At the supper last evening he had said, "This cup is the new covenant in my blood which is poured out for you."

In the garden, this very night, he had prayed, "Father, if you are willing, take this cup from me."

And now, before both his friends and his enemies, he said, "Shall I not drink the cup the Father has given me?"

The cup of suffering. The cup of wrath. The cup of God's will. Peter may have realized in that moment that he had got it all wrong. Though Jesus had been very clear that this journey he was on had only one outcome, Peter had stubbornly refused to accept that the road had always led to death, and not to the glorious military victory he had envisioned.

As though Jesus read Peter's mind, he continued, "Do you think I cannot call on my Father, and he will at once put at my disposal more than twelve legions of angels?"

Jesus had *a spiritual army* at his beck and call, but this was neither the time nor the place. The magnitude of this statement must have sent Peter's mind reeling. *Who was this man?*

The man who calmed the storm and walked on water.

The man who healed the sick and cast out demons.

The man who appeared in glory with Moses and Elijah.

The man who raised the dead.

The man who was served and strengthened by angels.

This man who stood before them now.

Jesus, the Messiah, the Son of God, Lord over all creation, commander of angels, Almighty and All-Powerful. In him, all things were created by him and for him, whether visible or invisible. He was before all things, in all things, and sustainer of all things.[78]

He was *not* a victim in this situation. He was not caught *off-guard* and *forced* to submit to his enemies. No. He was both wholly in charge, and wholly submissive to the will of his Father. His relationship with his Father was one of utter unity and love. What the Father desired, Jesus desired.

Peter should have recalled that Jesus had said his Father loved him because he was willing to lay down his life. He had said, "No one takes it from me, but I lay it down of my own accord. I have authority to lay it down and authority to take it up again. This command I received from my Father."[79]

Jesus was not *helpless*. Far from it. What transpired now was completely within the will of God, and it was Jesus' highest priority to fulfill God's will.

He had told Peter and the other disciples the previous evening, "I love the Father and do exactly what my Father has commanded me."[80] When Jesus prayed a little later, they heard him say to his Father, "I have brought you glory on earth by finishing the work you gave me to do."[81] For Jesus, everything he did was out of love for his Father and in obedience to his will.

The Father's will was not capricious. He did not want one thing one day, then change his mind the next. No, since before the creation of the world, the Father had a plan. Long before the first man and woman rebelled in the Garden, God had set in motion a plan for the restoration of mankind into a loving relationship with God.

Over the course of thousands of years, God's plan had been revealed in part through the prophets. To those with eyes to see, the path forward was visible. God would send a Savior, his own Son, to become a man and suffer to settle the debt incurred by man's sin. He would pay the ultimate price by voluntarily giving up his life. The Scriptures pointed to the coming of the Savior.

And now, with the soldiers ready to arrest him, and the crowds ready to kill him, Jesus pointed to the plan that had been unfolding since before time began:

"But how then would the Scriptures be fulfilled that say it must happen in this way?"

Peter knew the Scriptures. He believed God would send a Messiah. He believed Jesus was that Messiah. His mind grappled with a Messiah who dies versus a Messiah who reigns. It was too much!

Even the evil that grows in the hearts of men is used by God to bring His plan to its glorious fulfillment.

It's possible he remembered the parable Jesus told about the vineyard owner who left his tenants in charge of his property while he was away. The owner sent a servant to collect some of the fruit from the harvest, but the tenants beat the servant. He sent more servants, with the same result. Finally, he sent his own son to do what the servants could not, but the evil tenants beat the owner's son and killed him. Did Peter now realize that Jesus was the son?[82]

More likely, Peter was caught up in the moment and only thought about some of these things later, in the dark hours that lay ahead. At this moment, Jesus spoke to the chief priests and elders who came with soldiers to arrest him.

"Am I leading a rebellion, that you have come out with swords and clubs to capture me? Every day I was with you, sitting in the temple courts teaching, and you did not arrest me or lay a hand on me. No, you prefer to do things under the cover of dark. This is your hour—when darkness reigns. But this has all taken place that the writings of the prophets might be fulfilled."

Again, Jesus pointed to the plan of God. Even the evil that grows in the hearts of men is used by God to bring His plan to its glorious fulfillment.

Peter watched helplessly as the soldiers bound Jesus, the Jewish officials watching on with an air of arrogant triumph. They believed they had won their battle with this man who had disrupted their reign over the souls of God's people. Little did they know that the battle was just getting started. The victor had not yet been revealed to all.

As for Peter and the disciples, each of them gave in to the fear that rose up in their hearts. Fight or flight kicked in during the arrest. When fight was no longer an option, flight took over. All deserted Jesus and fled.

Did any remember their Master's words only a few hours earlier when he said to them, "This very night you will all fall away on account of me, for it is written, 'I will strike the shepherd, and the sheep of the flock will be scattered'"?[83] Did they remember their own indignant denials and protestations of innocence?

I can only imagine that at this point Peter is operating out of pure adrenalin. So much has happened over the past few hours. He had barely had any sleep save for the hour or two while Jesus prayed in the garden. Anxiety, stress, fear of the unknown, fear for his own safety, and the gut-wrenching realization that yet again he had let his Master down weighed on him like a man without hope. He loved Jesus but felt powerless to do anything. And so he ran.

We don't know how long he hid himself away. At some point that night, both Peter and John reconnected and decided to find Jesus, perhaps in the hope that he would be released, or only jailed temporarily. Things will grow far worse before they get better.

Personal Reflection

Think of a time when you were under an enormous amount of stress.

Perhaps you were dealing with the death of a friend or family member. Perhaps you found yourself suddenly without a job with mounting bills and a family to support. Perhaps a friendship you treasured experienced so much pressure that the relationship was no longer salvageable.

You reached out to God but did not feel his presence in your life. You felt alone and struggling.

What do you do when everything seems to have fallen apart and you feel helpless, grieved, and alone?

Do you try to remember better times, when God felt near, and life was happy?

Do you choose to persevere and continue to make right choices even though you'd rather just stay in bed?

Do you stuff all the bad emotions in a small dark closet, put on a fake smile, and find pleasure in other resources?

Do you lash out and hurt others, just to keep from having to feel the hurt within your own soul?

What do you think you would have done in the garden that night when Jesus asked you to watch and pray?

What do you think you would have done when you saw the soldiers and teachers of the law approaching to arrest Jesus?

What do you think you would have done when you realized your friend and fellow disciple Judas had betrayed not only your Master, but you as well?

We all experience trauma at some point in life. The strength of our dependency on God will determine how we respond.

Sometimes, God lets us see and experiences our weaknesses, so that we can learn to turn to him and trust his will for our lives. Sometimes, because of his grace, we choose what is right, encouraging others to do the same.

Peter is approaching the pivotal moment in his walk with God. His opportunities are not over. But the way ahead looks bleak. He is losing confidence in his own ability to follow his Lord in the right way. He keeps on making serious mistakes. Will he ever get it right?

---

[78] Col. 1:16-17.

[79] John 10:17-18.
[80] John 14:31.
[81] John 17:4.
[82] See Luke 20:9-18.
[83] Matt. 26:31; Zech. 13:7.

My Journal

Chapter 11

The Denial

*After a little while,
those standing nearby came
up to Peter.
"Surely you are one of them,"
they said, "for your accent gives
you away."
At that he began to curse and
swear to them,
"I do not know the man!"
And immediately a rooster
crowed.*

Matthew 26:73-74

Read First:

Matthew 26:57-75; Mark 14:53-54, 66-72; Luke 22:54-62; John 18:15-18, 25-27

I became a follower of Jesus Christ during my second year of college. My conversion experience was a dramatic turning point in my life. Not having grown up in a church or with any kind of religious background, I was overwhelmed with gratitude for my salvation as well as filled with joy whenever I read the Bible. I covered my car with bumper stickers proclaiming my new faith. I was a new person in Christ!

Not long after, I remember standing in the check-out line at the little grocery store across the street from my campus. A young man operated the cash register, checking people out. When it was my turn, the young man looked at me and said, "Who touched you?"

For a moment I was confused. *What did he mean?* He must have noticed my confusion because he then gestured to my T-shirt, bright red with a large white fingerprint and the words, "He touched me" emblazoned across the front.

He repeated his question. "Who touched you?"

I gave an embarrassed laugh and hoped acting like we were sharing an unspoken understanding would get me out the door without having to answer him. No such luck.

"Seriously," he repeated. "Who touched you?"

I stood there, momentarily unable to speak. All within the space of a second or two, so many thoughts raced through my mind as a huge surge of adrenaline flooded my body.

I did not want to answer his question. I wanted to leave.

At the same time, I knew that I was giving in to fear—fear of rejection, fear of being ridiculed, fear of being "weird." I'm sure my face turned six shades of red as the dreaded word stumbled out of my mouth.

"Jesus."

The clerk smiled. "I just wanted to see if you would admit it."

He finished checking out my groceries and I left. He probably didn't give it a second thought, but I was absolutely mortified, embarrassed, ashamed of myself and frankly, angry at the cashier for putting me in a very awkward position.

But why? Why was it so hard to admit with my words what I had no problem wearing on my shirt or sticking on my car?

That was my first encounter with the temptation to deny my Lord. I cannot claim any righteousness on my part for finally answering "Jesus" to the cashier. I basically tripped over my own feet and landed flat on my face in the right direction. That's the grace of God. In that moment, he showed me the fickle nature of my own heart, without letting me suffer the shame of outright denial.

The God of U-Turns

There are times in life when each of us approaches a crossroads of sort. We have a choice to make. Which road will we take? Will we continue traveling down the path we are on, or will we turn to the left or the right?

On another occasion, a couple years later, I was asked to help with a church event. I agreed yet proceeded to procrastinate until the event was less than a week away, and I *still* hadn't done my part. At church that Sunday, I tried to avoid the event leader who had asked me for help. No such luck.

When she asked if I had completed my task, panic set in, along with a million thoughts that seemed to take only a second to pass through my mind. I didn't want anyone to know that I had failed. I still had time to fix this. No one will ever know if I don't tell them. So, I reacted out of fear and lied.

"Yes, I completed the task," I told her, already strategizing to finish it as soon as I got home that day. I started to back away, but my leader proceeded to thank me profusely for helping. I mumbled something like "you're welcome" and hastily made my way toward the exit stairwell.

I had not made it more than a few steps down when I was stopped dead in my tracks by a loud voice in my head: "If you take one more step, you will start down the path to destruction." I couldn't move forward. I knew beyond any doubt that I had to turn around and make things right with the event leader.

With fear and trembling, I found her and asked forgiveness for being irresponsible and then lying to cover up my sin. I committed to finishing the task that day. She forgave me and the task was taken care of immediately. But the lesson I learned that day has stayed with me all these years.

Sometimes when we come to that crossroads, we choose the correct path immediately and continue to walk in trust and obedience. Sometimes we cave in to our own self-serving desires and choose the wrong path. The great thing about God is that he is the God of U-turns and second chances. His mercies are new every morning![67]

Peter was also facing a crossroads.

When he fled with the other disciples at the arrest of Jesus, he was not about to be arrested. He had not been charged with any crime. Striking the high priest's servant would have warranted some sort of intervention by either the soldiers or the guard, but Jesus immediately healed the wound. Jesus himself said to the soldiers, "If you are looking for me, then let these men go."

Why did he flee? This was not the action one would expect from someone one who had just hours before declared, "Even if all fall away on account of you, I never will. I am ready to go with you to prison and to death!" What happened to the confident leader of the Twelve?

I try to imagine myself in Peter's position. I try to recall how he struggled every time Jesus brought up his impending suffering and death. I remember how thrilled he was when he saw his glorified Lord with Moses and Elijah on the mountain. I hear how often he proclaimed his own loyalty and faith before others. And I wonder if his persistence in this was actually rooted in his own doubt and insecurities about his faith. Sometimes we think if we can say something loudly and confidently enough, it will be true.

Perhaps his faith was wholly placed in a certain type of Messiah. When Jesus lived up to that picture in Peter's mind, Peter felt optimistic and secure. When Jesus said or did anything that seemed to contradict Peter's vision of the Messiah, Peter became conflicted, trying to control his Master and mold him into the Messiah Peter wanted him to be.

Of course, this is all mere speculation.

We must remember that Peter was exhausted, struggling with fear, concerned for his Lord's safety, and discouraged by the many times he had either failed Jesus that night, or been rebuked by him. Then he had witnessed the shocking betrayal of Jesus by one of their own.

Also, when he tried to act by striking out with the sword, he was stopped by Jesus.

Finally, *all* the disciples fled: John, James, Andrew, Matthew, Thomas, Thaddeus, Philip, Simon the Zealot, Bartholomew and James, the son of Alphaeus. One might dare to stand against evil when surrounded by like-minded friends who have your back but seeing all your friends run away will sap the courage of most.

Following From a Distance

Peter was emotionally and physically spent. What more could he do?

He did not flee for long. At some point, perhaps even minutes after leaving, he stopped. Along with John, Peter changed course. He decided to follow the arrest party to keep watch over what was happening with Jesus. We know that he was still apprehensive because he kept his distance, staying far enough back so that he would not be detected by the soldiers or the crowd.

Peter and John followed the group to the residential palace(s) of Annas and Caiaphas in Jerusalem. Annas had been the high priest for years but was recently replaced with his son-in-law Caiaphas. It is unclear whether they resided in the same palace, or two palaces close enough to each other that Jesus could easily and quickly be moved from one to the other during the course of his interrogation.

When Peter and John arrived, it was around midnight. John had connections with those in the high priest's household and was readily admitted into the courtyard of the palace. Peter waited at the door while John spoke to the doorkeeper, who then allowed Peter to enter.

Jesus was already being questioned first by Annas. When Annas found nothing useful, Jesus was then presented to Caiaphas. John left Peter in the courtyard in order to find out more about what was happening to Jesus.

Peter initially tried to stay away from the soldiers and servants that were in the courtyard. However, a servant girl who was watching the door came up to Peter. She peered at his face and said,

"You aren't one of that man's disciples too, are you?"

To avoid drawing attention to himself, Peter lied. "I am not," he stated.

In the distance, a rooster crowed, but Peter did not pay attention to it. He was too preoccupied with his own safety.

The chilly courtyard was open to the night sky. Peter pulled his cloak tighter around him as he waited for John to return with word about Jesus. Some of the servants and officers had kindled a fire in the middle of the courtyard. Peter edged closer to the fire to warm himself.

Before long, some of those at the fire began glancing in his direction. "Aren't you also one of his disciples?" they asked. Peter pretended not to hear, but their words caught the attention of a passing servant girl who stopped and looked at Peter as the firelight reflected off his features.

"You *were* with Jesus," she declared. "I remember seeing you!" Peter responded in a hushed yet angry voice, "I am not," he denied for the second time. "I don't know him!"

Quickly, Peter moved away from his accusers and the fire. Time passed slowly. Around 3 a.m., he was once again recognized. A relative of the man whose ear Peter had cut off (and Jesus had healed), noticed Peter in the shadows.

"Didn't I see you in the garden when they arrested Jesus?" he asked. Peter denied it. But others standing around heard Peter speak, noting his accent. "You are a Galilean!" they stated, staring hard at Peter. "Surely you are one of his disciples—your accent gives you away!"

At this, Peter caved in to his baser nature. He let all the frustration and fear and anger that had been building up inside him pour out in a stream of curses and profanities. He shouted at them, "I don't know this man you are talking about!"

As he was speaking, the rooster crowed for the second time.

Peter looked up in time to see Jesus, shackled and bleeding, being led by the soldiers through the courtyard to another location. Jesus turned his head and looked straight at Peter, as the crowing stopped. Only then did Peter remember the words of his Lord when he said, "Before the rooster crows twice today, you will disown me three times."

Horrified that Jesus had heard his words of betrayal, Peter stumbled out of the courtyard and collapsed on the ground. Profound regret flooded his soul. He wept bitterly. Like one who looks at himself in a mirror for the first time, he recoiled in horror at the evil he saw in his own heart.

He remembered his calling from three years earlier, after Jesus had blessed his family with so many fish even after Peter had pretty much laughed in his face when Jesus asked him to throw out the net one more time. He had said then, "Go away from me, Lord. I am a sinful man." But now he knew the depth of his own depravity went far deeper than he had ever thought possible.

What had happened?

Peter dreaded not being "liked" and accepted. He was always the life of the party and enjoyed having people look up to him, laugh at his jokes, seek out his company. He was a born leader, persuasive and charismatic. He naturally attracted friends, so much that he came to depend on his reputation as a sort of personal security blanket. Peter was happiest when surrounded by people who liked him.

Because we tend to think of ourselves more highly than we ought, we are often shocked by even a glimpse of our sinful nature. But Jesus sees the deepest recesses of our hearts, and he is not shocked or repelled.

Over the past three years, as he walked with Jesus throughout the countryside with the other disciples, he felt like he belonged. He also recognized that he had been given an honor not bestowed to most of the others. He was part of the top three that his Master depended on the most.

Peter, James and John were privy to certain events that the others were not: the raising of Jairus' daughter from the dead, the transfiguration of Jesus on the mountain with Moses and Elijah, and the special invitation to watch and pray with Jesus in the garden at Gethsemane just the evening before. And he was the only disciple who had received a new name from Jesus. Peter, the Rock.

The Twelve disciples had been like brothers to him. They worked together as a team. Even when they had disagreements, or engaged in petty arguments, they still loved each other and supported each other.

They were bound together by their love for Jesus and their belief that he was the Messiah.

As Jesus' popularity grew, Peter's own popularity grew as well. Being recognized as one of Jesus' disciples, at least in the early days, was an honor. Peter felt special and singled out. However, as opposition grew to Jesus' ministry, the disciples felt the tension. Many followers left Jesus when they found his teachings too difficult. But the Twelve stayed, and Peter was considered their leader—after Jesus, of course.

But now, the others had fled. Peter was alone.

Even as he hid out in the courtyard among the officers and servants, awaiting news of Jesus' fate, he couldn't bear to stand alone. When asked if he knew Jesus, he succumbed to his natural tendency to do or say what would garner him more friends and fans, or at the very least, fewer enemies.

Peter struggled to take a stand against public opinion. He had always preferred to play for the winning team. So, he denied knowing Jesus out of fear of being ridiculed or laughed at or ostracized. The man who swore he was willing to die for Jesus, may also have denied him out of fear of physical punishment or death. Now the truth of who he really was inside lay visible to him and he was utterly ashamed and left weeping bitterly in the cold night air.

The Heart of Every Man

We see this tendency in Peter throughout the gospels, and even in his ministry *after* Jesus' resurrection and ascension. Paul, a man once hostile to Christ-followers who later became a believer, wrote much of the New Testament. In one of his letters, he wrote about an incident he faced with Peter.

Peter was staying in Antioch, where a church had been established with many Gentile (non-Jew) believers. He regularly ate meals with the Gentile believers until a group of Jewish believers traveled to Antioch to visit. When they arrived, Peter stopped eating with the Gentile believers, knowing the new group would not approve. Paul saw this people-pleasing tendency in Peter and called him out on his hypocrisy. Peter then repented of his actions.[68]

The thing that encourages me is, no matter what our tendencies or inclinations, Jesus is never surprised by the depth of our sin. Because we tend to think of ourselves much more highly than we ought, we are often shocked by even a glimpse of our sinful nature. But Jesus sees the deepest recesses of our hearts, he knows all our blackest thoughts, he recognizes the vilest motives within us. And he is not shocked or repelled.

From the beginning, Jesus has known what is in the heart of every man.[69] When the teachers of the law harbored critical thoughts about him, Jesus immediately "knew in his spirit" what they were thinking, and said, "Why are you thinking these things?"[70] We see repeated many times in the gospels, "But Jesus knew what they were thinking...," "Jesus knew their thoughts...," "Knowing their thoughts...," "Knowing their evil intent...." [71]

Jesus also knew the hearts and read the thoughts of his own followers:

When Philip told Nathanael about Jesus, Nathanael was sitting under an olive tree. Later, when Nathanael met Jesus for the first time, Jesus said to him, "Here truly is an Israelite in whom there is no deceit." Nathanael humbly replied, "How do you know me?" Jesus answered, "I saw you while you were still under the fig tree before Philip called you." Then Nathanael declared, "Rabbi, you are the Son of God; you are the king of Israel."[72]

When an argument started among the disciples as to which of them would be the greatest, "Jesus, knowing their thoughts..." gave them a lesson in humility.[73]

When a large number of disciples abandoned Jesus mid-way through his ministry, Jesus was not caught off-guard, for he "had known from the beginning which of them did not believe and who would betray him."[74]

Even on the night he was betrayed, Jesus knew everything that was about to happen. "For he knew who was going to betray him" and "Jesus, knowing all that was going to happen to him..."[75]

After the resurrection, when Jesus asked Peter if he loved him, Peter confessed, "Lord, you know all things, you know that I love you."[76] After Jesus ascended into heaven, Peter led the disciples in a prayer with the words, "Lord, you know everyone's heart..."[77]

No, Jesus is not surprised. He knows our hearts, yet he still welcomes us, loves us, forgives us, and restores us. He knows exactly what we need. He had told Peter the previous evening,

"Simon, Simon, Satan has asked to sift you as wheat. But I have prayed for you, Simon, that your faith may not fail. And when you have turned back, strengthen your brothers."

The man who saw Peter's heart, and knew all he had done and would do, gave Peter the greatest gift in these words. First, he told Peter that he, the manifestation of God on earth, *prayed* for Peter that his faith would not fail.

Second, he provided Peter with amazing hope.

"When you have turned back, strengthen your brothers."

This statement alone showed Peter that God was for him, that the God who knows the future knew that Peter would turn back to follow him, and that the Creator of the universe had a future and a purpose for Peter.

The Moment of Reckoning

Throughout the gospels, we have seen both the highs and the lows of Peter's relationship with Jesus. Of those events recorded by the gospel writers, of whom Peter himself was a source, the lows seem to outnumber the highs. We see a gradual progression of sin, sometimes disguised by the appeal of his own compelling personality.

His self-confident attitude substituted for faith in his Lord and occasionally led him to not only disregard instructions from Jesus, but also to rebuke him.

His enthusiasm and vocal declarations of loyalty faded whenever he grew tired and fearful, leading him to succumb to the temptation to sleep rather than "watch and pray."

His desire to show himself worthy and prove himself to the Lord and the other disciples when he cut off the ear of high priest's servant, only showcased him acting out of emotional impulse rather than trust in his Master's example.

His strength and leadership skills crumbled when he saw the other disciples flee during the arrest of Jesus. His words, "even if all else desert you, I never will" would haunt him over the next days.

Finally, his outgoing charismatic personality, so charming to his friends and family, vanished when he no longer felt like he belonged. In the courtyard, when the walls of companionship crumbled around him, he resorted to the resources of his own heart: swearing, lying, and calling down curses as he denied the man he swore to love. In that moment of reckoning, Peter finally saw himself as Jesus had seen him all along. Yet Jesus had still chosen him and loved him.

The Lord *never* left Peter. On each occasion, it was *Peter* who left his Lord.

Personal Reflection

Have you ever been afraid?

Maybe it was monsters hiding under your bed or in the closet when you were a child.

Maybe you were harassed or ridiculed in your later school years.

Maybe as an adult, you were thrust in the middle of circumstances that you didn't want—failure on the job, the loss of a friendship, the death of a loved one.

Think about how you felt when you were truly afraid. How difficult did you find it to think clearly or rationally? What physical toll did you experience?

When you think about the circumstances Peter went through, which of Peter's reactions makes sense to you? Falling asleep in the garden? Fleeing from the soldiers? Denying the Lord?

We all mess up. None of us is totally free from our sinful nature. It is there when we wake. It walks with us through the day. It lies down with us when we sleep. The fact that the New Testament tells us repeatedly to keep on putting the sinful nature to death, shows that it is alive and active in our lives.

Like Peter, how have you given in to fear rather than trusting the Lord? Are you following from a distance?

How have you acted impulsively or emotionally rather than turning to the Lord and asking for his help or wisdom in a difficult situation?

How have you wasted an opportunity to acknowledge your Lord to another person who doesn't yet know him?

How has God shown you that he loves you, forgives you, and has a plan for your life?

_____

[84] Lam. 3:23-4.

[85] Gal. 2:11-14.

[86] John 2:24-25.

[87] Mark 2:8.

[88] See Luke 6:8; Matt. 12:25; Luke 11:17; Matt. 9:4, 22:18.

[89] John 1:47-49.

[90] Luke 9:46-47.

[91] John 6:64b.

[92] John 13:11a; 18:4.

[93] John 21:17.

[94] Acts 1:24.

My Journal

Chapter 12

The Renewal

Jesus asked a third time, "Simon son of John, do you love Me?"

Peter was deeply hurt that Jesus had asked him a third time, "Do you love Me?"

"Lord, You know all things," he replied. "You know I love You."

Jesus said to him, "Feed My sheep.

John 21:17

Read First:

Matthew 24:1-10, 16-18; Mark 16:1-20, Luke 24:1-10; John 20:1-10; 21:1-20

After spending the night being questioned by both Annas and the high priest Caiaphas, Jesus was brought before the Roman governor Pontius Pilate for further interrogation. Though he found Jesus guilty of no crime, the governor caved in to the demands of the mob outside his palace and ordered the execution of Jesus. Jesus was then beaten and whipped before he was taken outside the city gates to Golgotha, the place of execution. There he was crucified.

He hung on the cross for several hours. All four gospel writers record the last words spoken by Jesus.

Between noon and 3:00, the light of the sun died. Some believe a solar eclipse began at that moment. As the sky began to darken, Jesus shouted out the beginning of Psalm 22, "Eloi, Eloi, lema sabachthani?" which means, "My God, my God, why have you forsaken me?"[95] Those familiar with the psalm would have known that this psalm of David goes on to describe the very events that Jesus was experiencing in those moments as he hung on the cross. The psalm ends praising God.

In the midst of the darkness, Jesus said, "It is finished."[96] The work the Father had entrusted to him was now accomplished. The debt of sin was paid. He had defeated the powers of Satan and opened the door to the Kingdom of heaven.

When the darkness lifted at 3:00, Jesus shouted one final time, "Father, into your hands I commit my spirit!"[97] Then he gave up his spirit.

His lifeless body stayed on the cross until shortly before sunset when some of his followers secured permission to take his body and lay him in a tomb until the Passover was complete. Roman guards were placed at the tomb from Friday evening through Sunday morning to make sure no one tried to steal the body.

During all this time, Peter is not mentioned by name in any of the gospel accounts.

Where was he?

Luke provides a clue. Having later extensively interviewed witnesses of Jesus' life, he wrote about the minutes when Jesus breathed his last: "When all the people who had gathered to witness this sight saw what took place, they beat their breasts and went away. But all those who knew him, including the women who had followed him from Galilee, stood at a distance, watching these things."98

Peter may have been among this number standing "at a distance." Possibly he hid in the recesses, horrified at what was happening and the part he had played in the final hours of his Master's life, yet unable to stay away from the man he had loved with all his heart.

Jesus Appears to Peter and the Disciples

On Sunday morning, Mary Magdalene and some other women discovered the empty tomb. When an angel appeared to them announcing that Jesus had risen from the dead, the women found Peter and John and told them.

Peter and John ran to the tomb to see for themselves. Neither man understood what had happened to Jesus' body. They left Mary at the tomb and returned to the city. Then Jesus appeared to Mary. Later that day, Jesus also appeared to Peter. 99

This was the first time after Peter's denial of Jesus that the two met face-to-face. We have no record from any of the gospels of what transpired between the Lord and his troubled disciple. But what a meeting that must have been!

That night, Jesus appeared to his disciples who had gathered together. This was his first appearance to them as a group. His second appearance to the group occurred eight days later in Jerusalem. Jesus told the disciples to return to Galilee where he would come to them again.

They probably left soon after this second meeting, walking about 80 miles back to Capernaum, a three- or four-day journey. Only the gospel of John records what happened during Jesus' third appearance to the disciples in Galilee...

Once they arrived, they waited for Jesus. Peter's patience may have worn thin as they waited. He decided to get out and do something to fill the time.

Perhaps he remembered a teaching by his Lord shortly before his death, "Who then is the faithful and wise servant, whom the master has put in charge of the servants in his household to give them their food at the proper time? It will be good for that servant whose master finds him doing so when he returns."[100]

Peter announced to the others, "I'm going fishing."

"We'll go with you." Six disciples joined Peter for a night of fishing: Thomas, Nathanael, the Zebedee brothers, and two unnamed disciples. Maybe the others chose to stay home and sleep rather than join the all-night fishing trip.

Though they fished for hours, they caught nothing. Sound familiar?

When the sun came up, they saw a man standing on the shore. He called out to them, "Boys, have you caught any fish?"

They shouted back, "No."

The stranger then told them, "Cast the net on the right side of the boat and you will find some."

They did what the stranger said, and the net was so full of fish they were unable to haul it in. Peter must have been getting a strong sense of déjà vu about now. Perhaps the Lord was showing them how only when they relied on him, would they be fruitful in their work, whether fishing for fish or fishing for men.

On the Beach

John shouted what Peter was already thinking, "It is the Lord!"

Peter, always the man of action, grabbed his outer garment that he had taken off and dove into the water, leaving the other disciples to handle the boat, dragging the net behind them for the one hundred yards to the shore. Peter swam as fast as he could to the man on the beach who had already prepared a fire and was heating bread and fish upon it.

The other disciples reached the shore and came to the man also. "Bring some of the fish you have just caught," he told them. "Come, have breakfast," the man said to them.

None of the disciples dared to ask him, "Who are You?" They knew it was the Lord. Then Jesus took the bread and the fish and gave it to them to eat.

Jesus, the now risen Christ, prepared breakfast for his disciples. Just as he had served them at the Last Supper by washing their feet, now he served them breakfast. He humbly provided for them, meeting their needs.

When they finished breakfast, Jesus turned to Peter and looked him in the eye. This was Peter's "come to Jesus" moment. None of the gospel accounts tells us where the other disciples were at this moment. It is entirely possible they were right there, present for this conversation between Jesus and Peter.

Imagine being Peter. Memories of that last night of Jesus' earthly life are still fresh in his mind. They haunt him. He can hear himself saying in front of everyone how he would lay down his life for Jesus. Instead, he had denied knowing him three times. He was ashamed to look his Master in the face or to meet his eyes.

Jesus took the initiative and spoke first.

"Simon, son of John."

Jesus called him by his old name, the name he had three years ago before he gave up his livelihood to follow Jesus. Jesus had renamed him Peter. Since then, everyone called him Peter, or Simon Peter.

I imagine Peter feeling very humbled at this moment. It seemed like a *demotion*, one he knew he deserved. He felt as if any gains made in the three years that he followed Jesus were lost, and he must start over again from scratch. But it gets *worse*. Jesus then asked Peter,

"Simon, do you love me more than these?"

The question was simple enough but contained a world of meaning for Peter. What did Jesus mean by "these"? Was he referring to the fish before them, meaning "Do you love me more than your livelihood? More than your own personal needs?"

Or did he mean, "Do you love me more than these other disciples love me?" In other words, "You said not long ago that even if all my other followers abandoned me, *you* would not—that your love was greater than theirs. I ask you now, do you still believe that *you* love me more than *they* do? Even after denying me three times?

"Will you put me first over and above your need for approval and acceptance by others? Will I always be your Lord, and not only when you are liked, or accepted, or followed?

"Will you still love me when you are rejected by men, betrayed by them, ridiculed for your faith, and persecuted because of me, or will you cave in to the expectations and praise of others? Will you love me if it means losing all your friends and being alone? Do you love me that much?"

I think this latter interpretation is closer to the truth. And the truth stings.

Peter was very aware of how he had given in to the fear of man, how he had chosen to "fit in" with the people around him rather than remain loyal to his Lord the night he denied him three times.

The other disciples were also keenly aware of Peter's prior declarations of loyalty, how he had compared himself to them, saying, "Even if all fall away on account of you, I never will." By now, they had all heard what happened in the courtyard of the high priest. Could they trust this man moving forward? Could Peter ever be the leader that Jesus called him to be?

Peter phrased his reply carefully. He knew his prior outbursts of devotion had been rooted in his own arrogant pride, and he had suffered the terrible fall that had come as a result. Using a much milder form of the word "love" than Jesus had used, Peter spoke from a position of humility.

"Yes, Lord," he answered simply, without any emotional declarations or self-promotion. "You know I love you."

Peter's words conveyed his understanding that Christ alone could see his heart and knew him better than he would ever know himself. He refrained from adding "more than these," unwilling to compare himself to others. He had learned a measure of humility, having suffered the fall that comes from pride.

Jesus accepts Peter's response, replying simply, "Feed my lambs."

In these words, the Lord gave Peter a new beginning, renewing his original call to be a "fisher of men." His first task was to provide nourishment and training to those "lambs" or young believers who are new followers or will shortly come to the faith. Just as Jesus himself had fed and nourished his disciples after calling them, Peter was charged with continuing Christ's example in raising up a new generation of believers.

Then Jesus asked Peter a second time,

"Simon son of John, do you love me?"

Jesus repeated the question, this time leaving off the phrase "more than these," but still utilizing the stronger word for love, a love so strong that it would lay down its life for the loved one. Would Peter lay down his life for Jesus?

Peter remembered his prideful arrogant boast from their last supper before Jesus' arrest. "Even if I have to die with you, I will never disown you." Yet, that is exactly what he did.

So, once again Peter answered with a different word for love, a word that does not include the great lengths he would go to in order to demonstrate his love but rather chooses a word that reflects a more brotherly love, a devotion and affection for another.

"Yes, Lord," he answered again, "You know I love you."

Jesus once again accepts his reply, saying, "Shepherd my sheep."

Jesus now tells Peter how to relate to those who are further along in the faith. He must act as a shepherd, or one who protects the flock and cares for their needs, in addition to feeding or instructing them in the ways of the Lord.

Jesus then asked the question a third time, but he softened the word love, meeting Peter where he was at, utilizing the word for love that Peter had used in his first two answers.

"Simon son of John, do you love me?"

Peter was deeply hurt that Jesus asked him a third time, "Do you love Me?"

He was hurt because it appeared that Jesus doubted the sincerity even of Peter's brotherly affection towards him. Peter knew he had failed Jesus. He had become painfully aware that his heart was deceitful above all things and had even deceived him about the depth of his love for Christ.

He was grieved that even his affection towards his Lord might be questioned, yet he was aware that his own actions had created this doubt. He realized if he himself could not rely on his own understanding of his heart, how could the Lord? But Peter also realized that the Lord was not like other men...

"Lord, you know all things," he replied. "You know I love you."

And here, he appealed to Jesus' ability to see into the depths of men's hearts. *He* must be the judge of Peter's love. *He* must be the judge of Peter's faith. So, he submitted his heart to Christ's examination to know if Peter was truly repentant and ready to obey in humility and love. Jesus' answer gave Peter the encouragement he needed.

Jesus said to him, "Feed My sheep.

The Lord examined his heart and knew that it was not Peter's *faith* that had failed in that moment in the courtyard; it was his *courage.*

Whenever he failed, Peter repented and tried again. His perseverance in the face of failure was unstoppable. He never quit. Peter stands like a light shining in the darkness for any of us who have ever failed as a believer.

Jesus then laid out Peter's future for him.

"When you were younger, before following me, you did what you wanted. You dressed yourself; you walked where you wanted to walk. You were the master of your own life. You didn't answer to anyone.

"But you have changed. You have grown. These past three years have transformed you. You have struggled with this transition. You know that you are no longer that free young man who did whatever he wanted. You now belong to me. And you must live for me. The time is coming when you will be old. Someone else will dress you and lead you where you do not want to go."

Jesus laid out what loving him really meant. Not only would Peter *live* for Jesus, he would also *die* for Jesus.

After Jesus had said this, He told Peter, "Follow Me."

Three denials.

Three professions.

One renewal of Peter's call.

Perhaps Peter remembered at that moment a conversation he had with Jesus at the last supper. Jesus had said:

"My children, I will be with you only a little longer. You will look for me, and just as I told the Jews, so I tell you now: Where I am going, you cannot come.

"A new command I give you: Love one another. As I have loved you, you must love one another. By this everyone will know that you are my disciples, if you love one another."

Simon Peter asked him, "Lord, where are you going?"

Jesus replied, "Where I am going, you cannot follow now, but you will follow later."

Peter asked, "Lord, why can't I follow you now? I will lay down my life for you."[101]

Peter had not been ready then. He still loved himself more than he loved people or even his Lord. He still had before him a huge lesson in humility, self-awareness, and learning to trust wholly in his Master.

But despite his failings, despite his weaknesses, despite his lying, his boasting, his impulsive and irresponsible outbursts, despite his denial of his Lord in the time of his greatest need, Peter kept coming back. He kept following Jesus.

The man who leapt off the boat in the raging storm and sank beneath the waters trying to reach Jesus, was also the man who jumped off the boat that day in Galilee when John announced it was Jesus was on the shore.

Peter saw the big picture. He finally realized that being a disciple of Jesus was not about *Peter* and what *he* wanted. It was about *God* and what *he* wanted. It was about *people* and what they *needed*. It was about realizing that God was committed to transforming all of us into the image of his Son, *despite* our failures and weaknesses.

Personal Reflection

As an old man, Peter wrote a letter to several churches to encourage them. Can you hear Peter's own experiences of being sifted like wheat in these words he wrote so many years later?

"Humble yourselves therefore under God's mighty hand, that he may lift you up in due time. Cast all your anxiety on him because he cares for you.

"Be alert and sober-minded. Your enemy the devil prowls around like a roaring lion looking for someone to devour. Resist him, standing firm in the faith, because you know that the family of believers throughout the world is undergoing the same kind of sufferings.

"And the God of all grace, who called you to his eternal glory in Christ, after you have suffered a little while, will himself restore you and make you strong, firm and steadfast. To him be the power for ever and ever. Amen."[102]

After Peter had suffered a little while, Jesus restored him, making him strong, firm and steadfast.

How does Peter's life bring you encouragement or comfort?

If Jesus asked you, "Do you love me?" How would you answer?

If Jesus asked you, "Will you put me first over and above your need for approval and acceptance by others? Will I always be your Lord, and not only when you are liked, or accepted, or followed?" How would you answer?

If Jesus asked you, "Will you still love me when you are rejected by men, betrayed by them, ridiculed for your faith, and persecuted because of me, or will you cave in to the expectations and praise of others? Will you love me if it means losing all your friends and being alone? Do you love me that much?"

How would you answer?

One of Jesus' last instructions to Peter and his disciples before his death was to love one another in the same way he had loved them. "By this everyone will know that you are my disciples, if you love one another."

How are you showing love to those God has placed in your life?

In this lifetime, it is never too late to turn around. No matter how far we have drifted, we are never so far away that Jesus does not see us and call out to us with open arms.

No matter what we have done, he says, "Come to me and I will give you rest." Peter's years with Jesus taught him to lean not on his own understanding, but to wholly trust in the one who saw his heart and still died for him.

Through trial and error, and failure after failure, Peter grew into the man Jesus had seen all along from their very first meeting. Whenever Peter failed, he repented and tried again. His perseverance in the face of failure was unstoppable. He never quit. Peter stands like a light shining in the darkness for any of us who have ever failed as a believer.

---

[95] Matt. 27:46; Mark 15:34.

[96] John 19:30.

[97] Matt. 27:50; Luke 23:46.

[98] Luke 23:48-49.

[99] Luke 24:34.

[100] Matt. 24:45-46.

[101] John 13:33-37.

[102] 1 Pet. 5:6-11.

My Journal

Appendix A

Why aren't the four gospel accounts more alike? Why does one writer include a description of Jesus' birth and childhood, while another says nothing? Why does one gospel writer describe an event with in-depth detail while another writer will not even mention it? For example, why do all four writers speak of Jesus walking on water in the midst of a storm, but only John relates Peter's attempt to do the same before sinking beneath the surface?

Understanding each author's audience and agenda is key.

Matthew's gospel focuses on a Jewish audience. Therefore, Matthew includes many references to the Old Testament and how Jesus fulfilled the prophecies of a coming Messiah made by the prophets of old. He also includes specifics about Jewish traditions and practices that would not resonate with readers unfamiliar with the Hebrew faith.

Luke, on the other hand, was a doctor and a Gentile. His gospel was written to persuade non-Jews that Jesus was the Son of God. He therefore focuses on the miracles of Jesus. The times he healed were also of particular interest to Luke, being a physician and familiar with the common maladies of times. He includes accounts of Jesus reaching out to those on the fringes of society, similar to the station many Gentiles found themselves in. He does not spend a lot of time on Old Testament prophecies because his audience would not be familiar with Jewish history.

John's gospel was written last, when John was an old man and the church was undergoing persecution. He writes to encourage believers, both Jewish and Gentile, emphasizing Jesus as the divine Son of God who provides eternal life to all who turn to him. He also tends to cover events not written about by the other gospel writers—no need to repeat events sufficiently covered already. His message through his gospel is one of hope, in a world that was harsh and severe to those who followed Jesus.

Mark's gospel was likely the first gospel written. In comparison to the other three, Mark's gospel seems abrupt. Sentences are shorter. Words and phrases like "immediately" and "right away" and "at once" pepper his narrative. A sense of urgency permeates his account, perhaps due to the early belief that Christ was returning at any moment. Mark writes to new believers, both Jewish and Gentile, and he emphasizes Jesus' power over sickness, death and the demonic.

Each gospel writer writes from his own perspective, with his own agenda, to his own unique audience. As we approach the Scriptures, bear in mind who the writer is, who his audience is, and what is most important to him.

Appendix B

Questions often arise after reading the gospel accounts of the morning of the resurrection—do the accounts conflict one another? How are the gospels trustworthy when the gospel writers cannot seem to agree on several of the details?

There is only one truth. Since the Scriptures are God-breathed, we trust that each account is part of that one truth.[104] We must always remember that we are not reading a minute-by-minute playback of everything that happened. We are reading one man's account to his particular audience. Apparent "contradictions" occur in appearance only. We simply don't see the whole picture.

Even the four accounts of what happened after Jesus rose from the grave on Easter morning can be harmonized. Did one angel or two angels appear to the women at the tomb? In fact, how many women were actually present? Did Mary tell the disciples what she saw, or did she keep quiet? We weren't there, we do not know for certain what happened—but we know enough to see possible avenues for harmonization.

The gospels accounts begin essentially with the same details. Here is a brief summary:

Early on the first day of the week while it was still dark, Mary Magdalene and several other women bought spices so that they might go and anoint Jesus' body. On the way, they asked each other, "Who will roll the stone away from the entrance of the tomb?"

When they arrived, they found the guards gone and the stone rolled away from the entrance. When they entered the tomb, they did not find the body of Jesus. Instead, they saw a young man in a white robe sitting. Suddenly two men in clothes that gleamed like lightning stood beside them. The women were terrified.

"Do not be afraid," the men said, "You are looking for Jesus, who was crucified. He is not here; he has risen! Go quickly and tell Peter and the other disciples, Jesus has risen from the dead, just as he told you!"

Then Matthew's gospel tells us that the women "hurried away from the tomb, afraid yet filled with joy, and ran to tell his disciples. Luke's gospel simply says, "they told all these things to the Eleven and to all the others." Mark's gospel, however, tells us that the women were both "trembling and bewildered" after speaking with the angel. They fled from the tomb and said, "nothing to anyone, because they were afraid."

How do we reconcile these accounts?[105] Here is one possible rendering that retains the facts of all the gospel writers. It is possible that the women initially were afraid and hesitated to tell anyone. But, after considering the words of the angels and remembering the words of Jesus, joy overcame fear, and they ran to tell the disciples. They found Peter, John and maybe a few others first. Mark's gospel says that "they did not believe the women, because their words seemed to them like nonsense."

John's gospel says, Mary "came running to Simon Peter and himself and said, 'They have taken the Lord out of the tomb, and we don't know where they have put him!" Her use of the word "they" probably referred to the guards, since they had left their post.

But why would Mary say she didn't know where Jesus' body was when the angels had clearly stated "He is not here; he is risen"? We don't know how Mary was interpreting the concept of being risen. She had seen Lazarus rise from the dead. His body walked out of the tomb. Jesus' body was nowhere to be found. Did someone take him home? Did the guards have him?

When Peter and John heard Mary's account, they ran to the tomb. John arrived first, looked inside and saw the strips of linen lying there. When Peter arrived, he walked straight into the tomb. He also saw the strips of linen lying there, as well as the cloth that had been wrapped around Jesus' head, lying separate from the linen. John followed behind Peter.

John's gospel says that John "saw and believed" but that neither understood from Scripture that Jesus had to rise from the dead. Peter exited the tomb, "wondering to himself what had happened." Then, both men returned to where they were staying, leaving Mary at the tomb.

Now Mary stood outside the tomb crying. As she wept, she bent over to look into the tomb and saw two angels in white, seated where Jesus' body had been, one at the head and the other at the foot. They asked her, "Woman, why are you crying?"

"They have taken my Lord away," she said, "and I don't know where they have put him." At this, she turned around and saw Jesus standing there, but she did not realize that it was Jesus.

He asked her, "Woman, why are you crying? Who is it you are looking for?"

Thinking he was the gardener, she said, "Sir, if you have carried him away, tell me where you have put him, and I will get him."

Jesus said to her, "Mary."

She turned toward him and cried out in Aramaic, "Rabboni!" (which means "Teacher").

Jesus said, "Do not hold on to me, for I have not yet ascended to the Father. Go instead to my brothers and tell them, 'I am ascending to my Father and your Father, to my God and your God.'"

Mary Magdalene went to the disciples with the news: "I have seen the Lord!" And she told those who had been with him and who were mourning and weeping. When they heard that Jesus was alive and that she had seen him, they did not believe it.

Placing Mary's encounter with Jesus here is consistent with Mark's claim that Jesus "appeared first to Mary Magdalene, out of whom he had driven seven demons."[106]

What about the other women?

We know that at some point after they left the tomb, and after Jesus appeared to Mary, he also appeared to the other women. Matthew says, "Suddenly Jesus met them. 'Greetings,' he said. They came to him, clasped his feet and worshiped him. Then Jesus said to them, 'Do not be afraid. Go and tell my brothers to go to Galilee; there they will see me.'"

But Luke's gospel tells us Jesus also appeared to both Peter and a couple of other disciples that day.

Now that same day, a disciple named Cleopas and his companion were walking in the country going to a village called Emmaus, about seven miles from Jerusalem. They were talking with each other about everything that had happened. As they talked and discussed these things with each other, Jesus himself came up and walked along with them; but they were kept from recognizing him. He asked them, "What are you discussing together as you walk along?"[107]

Cleopas and his companion relayed the events of the past few days, and how they had hoped that Jesus was the Messiah. They then described the events of that morning, before they had left Jerusalem.

In addition, some of our women amazed us. They went to the tomb early this morning but didn't find his body. They came and told us that they had seen a vision of angels, who said he was alive. Then some of our companions went to the tomb and found it just as the women had said, but they did not see Jesus.[108]

At this point, Jesus explained to them from the Scriptures all the prophecies concerning himself. Their hearts burned as he opened up their eyes to understand the passages. As they ate together that evening, they recognized Jesus only to watch him vanish before their eyes.

Immediately, they rushed back to Jerusalem. Once they found the disciples, they told what had happened on the road. The Eleven were overjoyed to confirm the news that yes, the Lord had risen and that he had appeared to Simon![109]

When had Jesus appeared to Peter?

Sometime after Mary, but before the women and the disciples on the road. Quite possibly, after Peter left the tomb, he encountered Jesus on his return trip into the city.

What a meeting that must have been but we have no record from any of the gospels of what transpired between the Lord and his troubled disciple.

I imagine a joyous reunion, but maybe not the complete reconciliation that needed to take place. If all was made right in this initial encounter, John's account of their later meeting in Galilee would not make complete sense. Maybe at this first appearance to Peter, Jesus told him essentially what had been said to Mary—that he had risen and that they should prepare to meet him in Galilee.

Later that night, Jesus appeared before all his disciples (except Thomas) at the same time. He ate with them and explained how everything that had happened was necessary to fulfill the Scriptures.

This was his first appearance before the group and concluded the events of that first Sunday.

---

[104] 2 Tim. 3:16.

[105] Mitchell, Elizabeth. "The Sequence of Christ's Post-Resurrection Appearances." Answersingenesis.org.

[106] Mark 16:9.

[107] Luke 24:13-17.

[108] Luke 24:22-24.

[109] Luke 24:33-34.

www.ingramcontent.com/pod-product-compliance
Lightning Source LLC
LaVergne TN
LVHW020929090426
835512LV00020B/3281